W9-BXE-547

ILLINOIS CENTRAL COLLEGE
PN4121.P56
STACKS
Speech as commu
280878

Speech as Communication

Speech as Communication

David C. Phillips
Head, Department of Speech
University of Connecticut

Jack Hall Lamb
Associate Professor of Speech
University of Connecticut

Allyn and Bacon, Inc., Boston, 1966

Library of Congress Catalog Card Number: 66-16022

Printed in the United States of America

FOREWORD TO THE STUDENT

If you are to get the most out of studying this text, there are some things you should know about the authors' point of view.

This is a book about the role of speaking in communication. And you do communicate all the time. You attempt daily and sometimes hourly to affect others—to cause them to understand or accept an idea, or to act upon your recommendation. At times you do this in the more formal situations that are usually called public speaking. More often your attempts to communicate are less formal, give-and-take presentations in social situations, in meetings of organizations, in committees, or through leadership positions in business, education, or social activities. This book attempts to prepare you for both formal and informal situations, with an emphasis on the latter.

The projects at the end of each chapter suggest activities that may be used in or out of the classroom. Some of these involve analyzing various types of communication situations, some require you to determine an approach to a communication, and some ask you to plan a communication. Your instructor may ask you to present some of these activities so that they can be analyzed and commented upon by the class.

We should also say a word about the materials for thought and discussion at the ends of the chapters. These selections have been chosen for a variety of reasons. Some are intended to expand on the material presented in the chapter. They have been written over the past 2,500 years by men interested in the problems of communication. You will therefore find excerpts dealing with communication as it has been known in the past, by such names as "rhetoric" or "eloquence." Other passages have been included in order to show the significance of communication in a wide variety of disciplines in our own day. A few selections were chosen because they illustrated principles discussed in the chapters, and a couple mostly for fun. We hope that all of them will stimulate you to consider communication as an everyday activity to be carried on outside the speech classroom.

David C. Phillips
Jack Hall Lamb

ACKNOWLEDGMENTS

Any author's writing, like any individual's oral communication, is the result of many influences. Often the exact sources cannot be identified. This is true of most of the ideas in this book.

In one instance, however, a specific influence on this book can be identified. Professor David K. Berlo of the Department of Communications at Michigan State University was the first major influence on the authors' attitude toward what today is called communication theory. His influence is still paramount, although it has been modified by a wider acquaintance with the literature of the field and by our experience in adapting the materials to various teaching situations in recent years. Chapters 2 and 3 can be traced easily to Dr. Berlo's ideas, even though changes have been made and ideas added. This is not to say that he would agree with what is in this book. We have a feeling that he might not, for most communications people seem to believe that it is not possible to tie together the traditional ideas of speech making and the modern concept of communication. However, we are indebted to Dr. Berlo for opening our eyes to a new approach.

To the many colleagues, students, professors, and others whose influence is not so easily identifiable, our many thanks.

CONTENTS

Speech as Communication

The common fluency of speech in many men, and most women, is owing to a scarcity of matter and a scarcity of words, for whoever is master of language and has a mind full of ideas, will be apt, in speaking, to hesitate upon the choice of words.—Swift

WHY LEARN TO COMMUNICATE EFFECTIVELY?

Our modern society is constantly becoming more complex, more dependent for its functioning on a variety of human interrelationships. Increasingly, people must work together to accomplish their goals, and this cooperation necessitates greater skill in personal communication.

Some time ago, the businessman had a few, perhaps at most a hundred, employees. He knew them and they knew him; opportunities for talk about mutual interests and problems were common. Today, a company may have thousands of employees. The plants of the company may be spread around the world, turning out highly diversified products. Usually several levels of management are required. The executive may depend on marketing analysts to advise him on what the public wants, on research and development men for new ideas and production methods, on financial experts for cost figures and money matters. The progress of the company depends on communication among all of the elements in modern industry.

The engineer or scientist who formerly worked alone is now a member of a project group; he must work not only with that group but with other project groups within a company. Ideas must be sold to the financial officer, the production head, and the marketing specialists. The engineer may find that his future depends on his becoming a manager of other engineers or people with different backgrounds and training.

The farmer of many years ago raised his crops in comparative isolation, his face-to-face communication limited to infrequent visits to a neighboring farm or trips to town for supplies. He was the most rugged of the rugged individualists. The present-day farmer is in constant contact with others concerning problems of growing, feeding, and marketing. He frequently organizes with other farmers to achieve common goals relative to distribution, prices, and government controls.

The labor leader, even on the local level, is constantly involved in communication to obtain new members, to persuade members to attend meetings, to explain contracts to his colleagues, and in negotiation with management. The educator, who has always made his living by talking with students, finds himself on various committees that have considerable influence on the environment in which he works. The statesman must confer with leaders from his own and other countries.

The difficult project of sending a manned capsule into space required considerable communication among various groups. Communication between the men in the craft and others on the ground is necessary. Much of this communication is electronic in nature, but the debriefing of the astronaut and the hours of communication between the astronauts and the scientists and engineers cooperating on the project contributed immeasurably to the success of the program.

The importance of oral communication to the student can be shown by a simple observation of the situations in which he participates daily. His communication may include a conference with a professor, a committee meeting in which he seeks action from the group, a house meeting, the asking or answering of questions in class, seeking advice on a course or a college plan, a bull session, a date, and perhaps an interview with a representative of a company he wants to work for.

The need, then, for understanding and using effective methods of oral communication becomes obvious.

Some communication is nonverbal. Actions frequently indicate attitudes and feelings. A frown or a shrug, a handshake or a refusal to shake hands, being on time, opening a door for a lady—all communicate attitudes. Nonverbal signals of this type are highly effective, but their usefulness in daily communication is limited.

Much communication is written. From a simple one-sentence office memo to the greatest novel ever penned, written communication can convey information, feelings, ideas, and beliefs.

But most communication is oral. Studies have shown that as much as 90 per cent of communication time is spent in talking and listening. The convenience of speed, the advantages of interaction between two people, the benefit of direct questions and answers, and the ability to probe a topic at once to the desired end all favor the use of oral communication.

Communication—particularly oral communication—is vital for the accomplishment of common goals at all levels of human activity. If we are to be effective in such communication, we must understand and use the principles that lead to success.

THE IMPORTANCE OF COMMUNICATION

Many colleges and universities have conducted studies to determine what changes in the curriculum, if any, are desirable to prepare students better for the modern world. One such study was sponsored at Lafayette College by the Ford Foundation Fund for the Advancement of Education. Several committees were established, composed of Lafayette College professors and successful businessmen, engineers, lawyers, doctors, educators, and theologians. Each committee, after prolonged study, stressed the need for college students to study communications—making it in every case their *first* recommendation. In their final report, the total committee recognized "the almost universal need among college students for a more thorough background and training in the use of oral and written English. . . ."[1]

The Harvard report, *General Education in a Free Society,* also points out the importance of communication. Four abilities to be acquired through education are listed: (1) to think effectively, (2) to communicate thought, (3) to make relevant judgments, and (4) to discriminate among values. The report continues, "Each [of these attributes] is an indispensable coexistent function of a sanely growing mind."[2] The speech class not only is the best place to study methods of effective communication; it also affords an ideal situation for testing the effectiveness of one's thinking, the relevance of one's judgments, and the ability to discriminate among values. As a student analyzes a problem to determine what he wishes to communicate, states and supports his contentions, and defends his position against questions from the instructor and fellow students, certainly he is testing his thinking, his judgments, and his ability to discriminate values. The report concludes its discussion of communication with these statements:

> . . . we have a point to make: that language needs to be neither high learning nor high literature to be communication. What we have in mind is the language of the businessman writing a plain and crisp letter, of a scientist making a report, of a citizen asking straight questions, of human beings arguing together on some matter of common interest.[3]

One of the authors of this book once shared a speaking platform with a doctor who was on the staff of a leading eastern U.S. medical school. The doctor was reporting the results of

1 *Commission Reports of the Self-Study Program of Lafayette College* (Easton, Pa.: Lafayette College, 1953), pp. 2–3.

2 *General Education in a Free Society,* Report of the Harvard Committee (Cambridge, Mass.: Harvard University Press, 1950), p. 65.

3 *Ibid.*

an 18-month study of why some medical grants from foundations achieved desired results and others failed. His personal observation of many groups in action led him to the conclusion that the primary cause of failure was inadequacy of communication. He said that if the individuals involved could communicate with each other even though representing different disciplines, the activity was usually successful. However, if the men could not communicate effectively even though in the same or similar disciplines, the chances of achievement were relatively small.

A business executive stated it this way:

> When an executive develops an idea, he is halfway to performing a valuable service to his company and himself as well. The other half consists of getting the idea into action. The payoff comes, both for the company and the individual, when other people understand the idea, accept it, and put it into effect. This is true whether the executive is a top man, giving leadership to the whole company, or a subordinate making a report and a recommendation to a top man. A scholar or a technical expert can often work up good ideas. A good salesman can sell them. The man at the top, or the one heading for the top, should be able to do both if he's to be a real leader.[4]

The college student who has an idea that will assist the student body on his campus must induce others to act before the result can be achieved. The citizen who sees a problem in his community must motivate others to join in the common goal of eliminating the evil. The engineer who develops a better process, method, or instrumentation may see his idea die if he cannot gather support from others. The politician can introduce a bill in a legislative body, but its passage depends on the agreement of other legislators or a majority of the voters. In all such situations, communication is the key to accomplishment.

[4] Reprinted by permission of Wayne State University Press from Arthur W. Pearce, "Getting Action on Executive Ideas," in *How To Improve Business Communication,* ed. Spencer A. Larsen (Detroit: Wayne State University Press, 1950), p. 116.

BASES OF COMMUNICATION

A teacher of speech formerly began his classes with this admonition: "You learn two things in this class: (1) when to be silent, which is 90 per cent of the time, and (2) to say what you have to say effectively." You may question the accuracy of the percentages, but the idea behind this statement is important. Each individual has certain responsibilities concerning communication, and unless he is ready to accept those responsibilities, his best approach is to remain silent. He must have (1) enough knowledge of the subject under consideration to meet his needs and the ability to use this knowledge to arrive at tentative conclusions; (2) the ability to recognize when he has a valuable contribution to make; and (3) the skills necessary to make his communication as effective as possible.

Knowledge

You have many opinions, some of them quite strong. You have ideas about whether your education has done for you what you think it should, about the attitude of your parents and society toward the teen-ager, about whether you want to go into service, about what you want to see on television. A quick way to make you angry, however, would be to begin to question you closely for the reasons behind your beliefs. When we are forced to substantiate our opinions, we soon discover that we have accepted conclusions too easily, without assuring ourselves that we have sufficient information on which to base those conclusions.

However, knowledge alone is not sufficient. Many knowledgeable people are poor communicators because they do not take the time to analyze the application of their knowledge to a particular situation. Knowledge alone is not power; knowledge applied is power, and the application involves drawing conclusions from what has been learned. Knowledge concerning imports and exports of the U.S. and Europe, their manufacturing and agriculture, rates of economic growth, and allied information is the first step toward communication on the subject of a common market. However, until the implications of such knowledge in a given situation are analyzed, the information is of little use to the communicator. Thus a second important point to remember is that between knowledge and communication comes the major step of analysis to discover the ways in which our information bears on the topic. If this step were adequately performed, much of our speaking today would stop before it began.

Necessity

Although many people talk too much, there are other individuals who could make real contributions to various communication situations but who say little or nothing. This reticence may be caused by fear of speaking—not only in public but even in small groups. Some individuals who should speak and do not are over-conscious of the necessity for adequate information. We all know that there are many problems in daily life concerning which the evidence is incomplete and may always remain so. What should your college major be? Will you have time to hold this new campus office and still keep your grades up? Which job should you accept? What candidate for office will do the best job? The answers to these questions are not clear until after the decision has been made, and perhaps not even then, but the decision will have to be made on the basis of the evidence at hand.

Some individuals remain silent for fear of being misunderstood or misquoted. There is no question that misunderstanding is possible, particularly if the communication is garbled or weakly presented. However, remaining silent because of the fear of misunderstanding can lead to action by others that is ineffective or harmful. The answer is not to remain silent but to be as lucid as possible in order to reduce misunderstanding. If, after proper thought, a person concludes that he has something of value to contribute for clearer understanding or better action, he *must* communicate it and as dynamically and precisely as he can.

Aristotle affirmed his conviction that where truth and error are equally well presented, truth will prevail. Every individual who has something to add to what he considers the right side of a controversy has a responsibility to add it. It is only thus that we can be sure that truth will not suffer because its side was not presented as well as it should have been.

Effectiveness

It is obvious that much of the communication that goes on around us is inadequate. Businessmen, government leaders, educators, doctors, labor leaders, and many others report constantly in private conversations and in publications that communication is their major problem. The misunderstandings that take place, the number of times information must be repeated, and the questions asked that show a real lack of understanding of what has been said, prove the ineffectuality of much communication. H. A. Overstreet, a psychologist, sums it up with these words:

> Few in adulthood are able to say what they want to say with confidence, precision, beauty, and a sensitive awareness of what is fitting in the situation. . . . In no area of our maturing, in fact, is arrested development more common than in the area of communication.[5]

There are no 10 easy steps to effective communication. It is a hard and laborious route. There are no "keys" to easy success in all communication situations, no buttons you can press to bring a communication off successfully. There are, however, some principles that, properly applied, can assist any individual in being more articulate. Aristotle discussed some of these principles over 2,000 years ago, and many men since his time have devoted a major portion of their lives to the art of speaking well. The remaining chapters of this book are a

[5] H. A. Overstreet, *The Mature Mind* (New York: Norton, 1949), p. 54.

distillation of the thoughts of such men. When these principles are properly understood and applied, they can assist any individual who has knowledge, ideas, and a desire to be more effective.

CONCLUSION

The core of human activity is communication. We learn from the past by it. We determine our own activities and social customs through it. We influence others by it. Especially in today's world, the importance of communication must not be underestimated.

Before attempting to communicate, we should recognize the responsibility for gaining knowledge and using that knowledge to determine what we have to say, the responsibility for contributing when we have something of value to say, and the responsibility for being as effective as possible.

At the end of each chapter in this book you will find a set of review questions and a list of projects. The review questions are a check on your understanding of the content of the chapter. The projects generally suggest ways in which you can apply the principles discussed in the chapter. Some projects will have to be done in class; others are exercises that you can do on your own. You are not expected to attempt all of the projects. Your instructor may assign some of them, and you may wish to perform others to test yourself.

REVIEW QUESTIONS

1. What implications have the complexities of modern life for communication?

2. What three channels of communication do we use constantly?

3. What responsibilities must the conscientious speaker assume before he begins to communicate?

PROJECTS

1. The instructor or a member of the class should first draw five rectangles that touch each other. Here is one possible pattern:

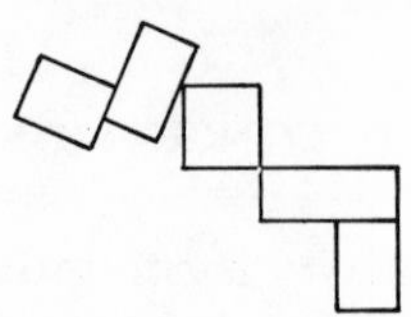

   The drawing should not be seen by the class. A speaker will then attempt to describe the positions of the rectangles, without using his hands, so that the members of the class can reproduce the drawing. The first time this experiment is tried, the class may ask no questions, and should attempt not to let the speaker know—by facial expression or other cues—what progress is being made. (If possible, the speaker might be seated at a table in the front of the room with his back to the class.) Repeat the experiment (with the speaker facing the class), this time permitting fellow-students to ask as many questions as they like.

   How many students reproduced the drawing accurately the first time? The second time? Account for the difference. What sort of things made the communication either effective or ineffective?

2. Keep a list of the communication situations in which you are involved during one day. Studies indicate that people in some occupations spend as much as 90 per cent of their working time in communication: reading, writing, listening, speaking. What percentage of your waking hours is spent in communication?

3. Discuss all of the kinds of communication that were involved in a job you have held. Without giving the matter some thought, you may leap to the conclusion that communication was not very important in your job. Let us give you a hint with which to begin: How did you first hear of the opening?

MATERIAL FOR THOUGHT AND DISCUSSION

Conversation in this country has fallen upon evil days. . . . It is drowned out in singing commercials by the world's most productive economy that has so little to say for itself it has to hum it. It is hushed and slushed in dimly lighted parlors by television audiences who used to read, argue, and even play bridge, an old-fashioned card game requiring speech. It is shouted down by the devil's advocates, thrown into disorder by points of order . . . subdued by soft-voiced censors.

Conversation . . . laid the foundation of the civilization we are dedicated to defend. It was conversation of which the New Testament, the greatest teaching ever recorded, was composed. . . . Great books, scientific discoveries, works of art, great perceptions of truth and beauty in any form, all require great conversation to complete their meaning; without it they are abracadabra—color to the blind or music to the deaf. Conversation is the handmaid of learning, true religion and free government. (*From a statement by A. Whitney Griswold, President of Yale University from 1950 to 1963, at the opening convocation of Brown University, September 1954.*)

The real intellectual life of a body of undergraduates manifests itself not in the classroom, but in what they talk of and set before themselves as their favorite objects between classes and lectures. (*Woodrow Wilson*)

One of the most distinguished privileges which providence has conferred upon mankind, is the power of communicating their thoughts to one another. Destitute of this power, reason would be solitary, and, in some measure, an unavailing principle. Speech is the great instrument by which man becomes beneficial to man; and it is to the intercourse and transmission of thought, by means of speech, that we are chiefly indebted for the improvement of thought itself. Small are the advances which a single, unassisted individual can make towards perfecting any of his powers. What we call human reason, is not the effort or ability of one, so much as it is the result of the reason of many, arising from lights mutually communicated, in consequence of discourse and writing. . . .

The study of rhetoric . . . supposes and requires a proper acquaintance with the rest of the liberal arts. It embraces them all within its circle, and recommends them to the highest regard. The first care . . . to speak in public so as to command attention, must be, to extend their knowledge; to lay in a rich store of ideas relating to those subjects of which the occasions of life may call them to discourse. . . . (*From the Introduction to* Lectures on Rhetoric and Belles Lettres by *Hugh Blair. Philadelphia: Matthew Carey, 1793, Vol. I, pp. 5–7. These lectures were first presented at the University of Edinburgh about 1760.*)

❖❖❖❖

The first essential is that the speaker should have something to say and be reasonably sure himself what that something is. Most speakers have an emotion, a prejudice, a slogan, some facts, or even an idea which they want to impart. But many of them do not develop their theme, whatever it is, logically, critically, or persuasively. They never listen to themselves and ask the essential questions: Is it so? And so what? Some speakers assume that because they have The Truth on their side, facts don't matter; others act as if the text "Out of the abundance of the heart, the mouth speaketh" absolved them from any use of their heads. More than once I have heard good men come out second best to demagogues in argument because they have depended on their righteous indignation and neglected their homework. (*Norman Thomas, "Random Reflections on Public Speaking,"* Quarterly Journal of Speech, *April 1954, p. 146.*)

❖❖❖❖

A number of years ago I had some experience with being alone. For two succeeding years I was alone each winter for eight months at a stretch in the Sierra Nevada mountains on Lake Tahoe. I was caretaker on a summer estate during the winter months when it was snowed in. And I made some observations then. As the time went on I found that my reactions thickened. Ordinarily I am a whistler. I stopped whistling. I stopped conversing with my dogs, and I believe that the subtleties of feeling began to disappear until finally I was on a pleasure-pain basis. Then it occurred to me that the delicate shades of feeling, of reaction, are the result of communication, and without such communication they tend to disappear.

A man with nothing to say has no words. Can its reverse be true—a man who has no one to say anything to has no words as he has no need for words? (*From* Travels with Charley in Search of America, *by John Steinbeck.*)[6]

I would say that the effective speaker is one who accomplishes what he sets out to do. To do that, he should know more about the subject than his audience. And he *must* believe what he is saying. These, in my opinion, are the two essentials. I can't emphasize too strongly the importance of getting the true facts; a man must know what he is talking about and know it well. As for sincerity, the public is quick to detect and reject the charlatan and the demagogue. It may be deceived for a brief period, but not for long.

In my opinion, mere talent without intellectual honesty and accurate information is not enough to make a successful speaker. I've never said anything in a speech that I did not firmly believe to be right. (*Harry S. Truman, quoted from Eugene E. White and Clair R. Henderlider, "What Harry S. Truman Told Us About His Speaking,"* Quarterly Journal of Speech, *February 1954, p. 39.*)

2

The talkative listen to no one, for they are ever speaking. And the first evil that attends those who do not know how to be silent is that they hear nothing.—Plutarch

THE COMMUNICATION PROCESS

Most of us probably think of communication as a single act in which one person speaks and another listens, with primary emphasis on the man who is talking. A brief look at a communication situation shows that this is far from the whole story. The listeners are also "speaking" while another is making his presentation. They bring with them their knowledge, attitudes, beliefs, and feelings, and because of their backgrounds they react to what is being said. These reactions may be either verbal or physical, but the communicator who is conscious of what is going on around him is aware of them.

Suppose, for example, that you attended a lecture last night on the problems of man in space. When you returned to the dormitory, your roommate, who had not attended the lecture, asked, "What did he say?" You are about to answer the question by telling him something that you learned.

As the speaker, or communicator, you have several means at your command by which to get your idea across. Your facial expressions, physical attitude, and gestures may help. You may draw a diagram on a piece of paper. But these are merely aids;

the main ingredient of your communication will be the words you choose to develop what you have to say.

Your roommate, the listener, can get some clues by watching you and looking at your drawings, but his primary means of understanding you is to think about the words you are using. He listens, and by attaching his own knowledge, experience, and attitudes to your words he attempts to derive meaning from what you say.

Thus, we have two participants in a communication situation, which we might diagram like this:

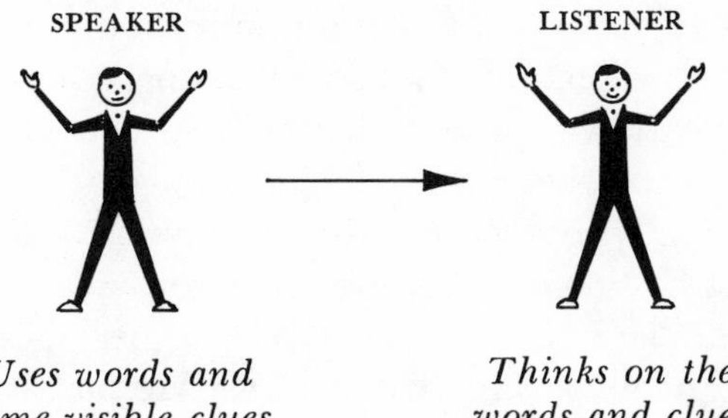

Uses words and some visible clues

Thinks on the words and clues

Important as these factors may be in communication, the process is not complete. Something must happen as a result of these two steps. If the listener lets the speaker's words "go in one ear and out the other," communication has not taken place. If the listener receives little or no meaning, or misunderstands the meaning, the speaker has not communicated effectively. But if a hearer understands what is being said, arrives at or changes a belief or attitude, or makes a decision, communication has taken place. The closer the result is to that intended by the speaker, the more effective the communication. Thus, the mere presence of two people, one using words and the other listening, does not make communication. The necessary third ingredient is the response. Communication is complete only when something changes as a result of the interaction of the two individuals. Our diagram would now look like this:

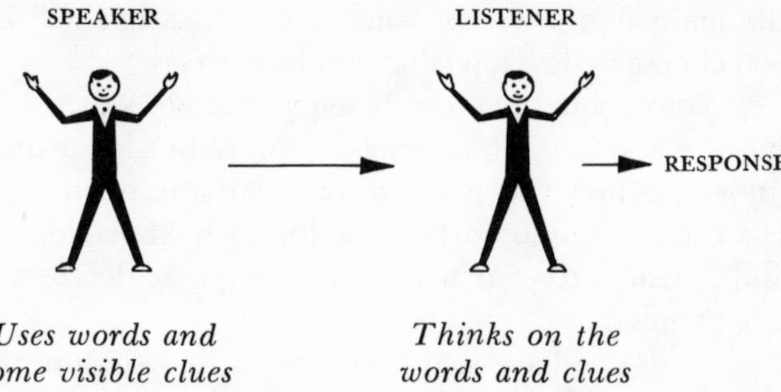

Uses words and some visible clues

Thinks on the words and clues

But even this diagram and explanation does not tell the whole story of the process of communication. While you are speaking, your roommate is also initiating communication to you. He may frown to show that he does not understand, and if you are perceptive you will add explanation so that the communication will be clear. By his physical attitude, he may indicate that he does not believe what you are saying, and you may wish to adapt to that signal. If he becomes inattentive, you can be quickly aware of that fact. He may actually interrupt your discourse with a quick question or comment. Thus both you and your roommate are constantly changing from speaker to listener and back again. On occasions you may be both at the same time. We could therefore repeat the diagram again, this time exchanging the names of the listener and the speaker.

This interchange is not limited to situations involving only two people. It takes place in all speaking situations no matter how many are present. Even in a formal speech with an audience of one hundred or more gathered to hear "a speaker," the listeners will be sending signals by nonverbal means, or in some situations by questions and comments. The signals from the audience may be varied and even conflicting, but failure to perceive them can mean failure to communicate.

It is not true, then, that a speech or a single communication is an isolated event where one individual "speaks" and others "listen." The measure of effectiveness is not how well the "speaker" conforms to a set of principles or techniques, but what response the listener makes. The accepted principles of communication are of considerable aid in achieving the desired goal; that is why we study them. However, they are the means to an end, not an end in themselves.

THE SPEAKER AND THE LISTENER

We have pointed out that communication is not an isolated event. Not only do the speaker and the listener constantly interchange roles, but each brings many things to the communication situation. His past experience, reading, and other communication has given each of them a certain amount of information about the subject at hand. These experiences may have led them to certain beliefs. They may have developed certain attitudes toward the topic, toward themselves, and toward the people present. These are other factors that have a great influence on what should be said, how it should be said, what response is possible, and what approach should be used. Most of these factors can be discussed under four headings: (1) knowledge, (2) attitudes, (3) communication skills, and (4) roles.

Knowledge

In the example that was used to open this chapter, the knowledge about space problems that both you and your roommate have will affect what you say about the lecture. You may have had considerable information about space matters prior to hearing the lecture, some of which you include for clarity in the communication with your roommate. If you are a novice in the area, you may omit certain things covered in the lecture because you did not understand them or cannot report them accurately. Your roommate's knowledge will also influence your communication. If he is a novice, full explanations may be necessary. If he is knowledgeable, you may make passing references to information that he already has. He may have a good background in some areas of the lecture, so that you omit those and concentrate on areas of more value to him. These are but a few examples of how the speaker's and the listener's knowledge will influence communication.

Attitudes

The attitudes of the individuals involved in a communication situation generally fall into three categories: (1) their attitudes toward the topic, (2) their attitudes toward each other, and (3) their attitudes toward themselves. Attitudes and methods of working with them will be discussed fully in Chapter 5, so a brief mention will suffice here.

In our space lecture example, your roommate may have little interest in the topic. You may decide, however, that he should know more, and thus make some opening remarks to spark his interest. Or you may just give a brief report of the lecture, having no desire to overcome his apathy. You may have little interest in the topic yourself; if so, you probably did little real listening and so have little to report. However, if both you and your roommate have a real interest in the space field, your report may be long and comprehensive, with many questions and comments from him. The attitudes of both the listener and the speaker influence communication significantly.

The attitudes you and your roommate have toward each other are also important. If your roommate has a rather low opinion of your ability to discuss space problems, you may find it difficult to interest him in your report. Your communication would be different if he respected your ability in this field. By the same token, if your attitude toward your roommate's knowledge of outer space is not very favorable, you will attempt to adapt your remarks to what you think his ability is in this field.

We cannot overlook the attitude that each person has toward himself. If your roommate has a rather high opinion of his knowledgeability, deservedly or not, you may have to be careful of the ideas you choose to develop, the words you use, and the completeness of your descriptions. If his opinion of his own ability in scientific fields is rather low, a different communication would be necessary even if the same ideas were to be expressed. If your opinion of your own ability either in the field of science or in communicating is low, he may have to ask more and specific questions to draw the proper communication from you.

It is impossible to discuss all of the various attitudes that may affect a communication situation. The important point is that these attitudes are brought to the situation and must be considered if the proper communication is to take place.

Communication skills

Both the speaker and the listener bring some ability in certain communication skills to the speaking situation. Such factors as the ability to listen, extent of vocabulary, ability to conceptualize, and need for visualization will influence what the speaker can do and what the listener can receive. You may know that your roommate listens well, thinks quickly, and sees relationships with ease. If this is the case, you can present ideas rapidly. However, if he misses ideas presented orally, is slow in seeing relationships, and needs time to comprehend, you may include more examples, make more detailed explanations, use more drawings, stop to ask him questions, and use other means to insure the success of your communication.

Roles

Each individual finds himself in various roles throughout an average day. Your roommate may be editor of the campus newspaper, a student interested in physics, a member of a military or anti-military group, a man facing military obligations. He may listen to your report in any one of these roles or any combination of them. He may, as editor, want a report for the paper. As a physics student he may be looking for the latest information. As a potential military man he may try to fit himself into some slot dealing with space, or if he is anti-military he might assume the role of advocate against space exploration that might lead to military uses.

The role he assumes as you speak may well influence what you say. If you know that he wants a report for the paper, you may be more cautious in your statements than if he were listening as a roommate. If you know that he is listening with the interest of a student of physics, a totally different communication might be made, stressing technical information.

You, too, may assume certain roles in your communication. You may be the anti-military person, so that he should be wary of bias in what you choose to report and how you report it. Your communication as "roommate" would be different from that as "newspaper reporter." Perhaps you listened to the lecture as a student in a speech class with a report due on an outside speaker. This would affect your later communication.

Every individual involved in a communication situation as both speaker and listener brings many influences to that situation. Your father plays various roles during his daily activities. For instance, when talking about education in your home community, is he speaking as a father interested in his son's becoming well educated, as a taxpayer worried about increased levies, or as a leading businessman trying to get along with other businessmen who may or may not be interested in education in your community? He is all of these people, and what he says in any given communication situation may be strongly influenced by whichever role he is playing at the time.

In a dormitory meeting discussing a coming social event, are you in the role of just a member of the group, a friend of the social chairman trying to recruit some help for him, or a member who recognizes that such an event will mean more work for you? You are all of these people, and the role that you are playing at any given time in the meeting will influence both how you receive what others say and what you will say yourself.

To ignore the knowledge, attitudes, communication skills, and roles that each participant contributes to communication is to risk failure in communicating. The situation is so complex that even a thorough study of each of these factors does not guarantee success. But if they are not taken into account at all, the chances of successful communication drop considerably.

DEFINITION OF COMMUNICATION

The discussion in this chapter has indicated thus far that the response a listener makes to a speaker is an important element in successful communication. This leads us to a definition of communication: *Communication is the seeking of a discriminatory response from a listener.*

Two words in this definition need further explanation: (1) discriminatory, and (2) response. Let us discuss them in reverse order.

The purpose of all communication is to elicit a response. This response may be on three levels: (1) understanding, (2) acceptance, (3) action.

The first step in communication is to make sure that your listeners understand what you are talking about. A student talking with a group of fellow students about a change in student government may first need to explain exactly how the present system works. A manager working with others to evaluate possible changes in personnel policies in the company may need to describe recent events that seem to have been caused by weaknesses in the present policies. An instructor in a seminar may need to explain the foreign policy of our government before applying it to the specific situation at hand. A student in speech class talking on censorship may need to review the laws affecting censorship. If you are sure that your listeners have an adequate understanding of the subject under discussion you may not begin on such an elementary level. However, it is seldom safe to assume that your hearers actually do understand, even when they themselves think that they do.

In a very few situations, understanding may be all that you seek, although most listeners are not likely to remember very much information that does not seem to apply to them. In most situations, you will be seeking understanding as a basis on which to build acceptance of an idea. Acceptance is the second level of response. The student talking with his colleagues about student government usually wants to make a change of some type or to obtain support for the present system. The manager presenting information concerning recent results of applying personnel policy generally desires some correction. An instructor discussing foreign policy as it applies to a certain situation often is either seeking agreement with the policy or pointing out possibilities for a more effective approach.

The ultimate goal of most communication is the third level of response—action. Immediate action is often impossible, of course, and so the speaker may stop when he has acceptance. However, he will want this acceptance to be so strong that when action is possible at a later time, it will take place. It may not be difficult to convince a student that an increased vocabulary would help him, but if the listener takes no action to amplify his vocabulary, the communication has had no effect. The same is true of communication concerning the changing of educational procedures, voting, attitudes toward the handicapped, and similar topics. The speaker must seek strong enough acceptance so that appropriate action will take place at a later time—often much later.

It is important to remember not to expect major changes as a result of a single act of communication. It may be advisable to seek a minor response at one time and to build on that response in the future. For instance, the ultimate response desired might be a whole new set of study habits for the listeners. The first step, however, may be to buy a book on the subject, or to plan regular study hours. One of these responses might be achievable, but the total response might be too revolutionary for the hearer to accept at one time.

The more specific and direct the response sought, the easier it will be for the listener to respond. The speaker who concludes with the plea, "Something must be done!" does not give his listeners much guidance. The speaker who throws out a plethora of specific responses such as, "Talk with your friends," "Bring it up in your house meeting," "Write a letter to the campus newspaper," and "Go to the administration and demand action," is usually just as ineffective. The careful choice of one desired response is the best procedure.

It is incumbent on the communicator to carry his listeners as far as he can with his efforts. Suppose that the topic is low grades. The speaker may go to the Registrar's office and the library and collect data on grades received by students in semesters one through eight, or he may gather the flunk-out figures for his and other institutions. If he merely reports these figures, he has done very little for his listeners. He might go further and determine the various reasons for low grades, and after proper preparation communicate the most important reasons as he sees them. He might achieve general agreement that these were the primary causes, but he still may have done little for his hearers. If, however, he goes one step further, and after determining the causes of low grades decides how his listeners can best overcome these problems, he is seeking a specific response. This can be a real contribution to his audience and can lead to the ultimate goal of most communication—to achieve in the listener the beliefs, attitudes, and acceptance that will eventually cause action.

The other word in our definition of communication that needs discussion is "discriminatory." At times the communicator cannot predict exactly what action should be taken because of the circumstances. You may be discussing student apathy with other students. Because they represent various organizations and have different goals in school, you cannot predict exactly what action each should take. But you can try to induce each listener to establish a set of values and procedures that are appropriate for himself and his group. In another situation you might discuss steps that would strengthen secondary education and each of your listeners might have to determine which of your suggestions apply to his community and what should be done first.

Thus, although the response that the speaker seeks should

be as specific as possible, there are many cases in which he cannot urge the listeners toward one particular action. In such cases he must rely on the discrimination of the listeners to make the proper decision.

AFTER COMMUNICATION, WHAT?

We have discussed the various influences and factors that individuals bring to a communication situation. We should not make the mistake of feeling that upon leaving it listeners depart into a vacuum. They may leave with a new understanding, belief, or even a commitment to action, stated or felt. Immediately, however, other things begin to happen to them. Other problems crowd out the urgency that they felt about what you had to say. Other people with different ideas and opposing points of view will communicate with them. Time and forgetfulness may erode your accomplishments.

It is important to take these factors into consideration when you are communicating. There may be an objection to your point of view that you were aware of but did not mention. When someone else brings this objection up later your listener will not have an answer. Make certain points especially vivid in order to overcome the tendency to forget. It is impossible for a speaker to predict all that can happen to affect the results of his communication, but the probabilities are there and must be taken into consideration if optimum communication efficiency is to be achieved.

CONCLUSION

It is important that the student of speech recognize that communication is a process, not a single act in isolation. The speaker and listener are constantly changing places while communication is going on. Both are sending and receiving signals—words and physical cues. That communication is a process means also that any single act of communication is built upon what the speaker and listener bring to the situation—their knowledge, their attitudes, their communication skills, and the roles that they assume.

Even what may happen after your communication must be considered before and during your presentation. If the proper response is to be gained, and that is the goal of all communication, you must prepare your listeners to maintain the beliefs and attitudes that you have persuaded them to adopt.

Communication is defined in this book as the seeking of a discriminatory response. The response can have three levels: understanding, acceptance, and action. We ordinarily desire action on the part of our listeners, and that action is often delayed. Thus our communication must cause the listeners to retain their understanding and acceptance until the appropriate time for action arrives.

REVIEW QUESTIONS

1. What is the essential test of whether communication has taken place?
2. What clues during a communication might tell a speaker how much his hearers know about his topic?
3. What attitudes of the speaker and the audience are important to the effectiveness of communication?
4. What are the communication skills?
5. What does it mean to say that a person plays many roles during the course of a day?
6. Define "communication."
7. What are the three levels of response?

PROJECTS

1. In a bull session in your dormitory, do not participate but instead spend your time answering these questions:
   (a) Does anyone seem conscious of and adapt in any way to what the others brought to the situation?

(b) What kinds of feedback are the listeners giving to any of the communication?
(c) Does anyone heed any of the feedback?

2. Analyze the communication process in a lecture in any of your classes:
   (a) Is there interaction between the instructor and any of the students? Why or why not?
   (b) What adaptations are made to the listeners' attitudes, knowledge, skills, and roles by the instructor?
   (c) What kinds of feedback are the listeners giving to the speaker? Is he adapting to them?

3. Remembering that you are communicating daily with various individuals and groups, can you recall communication situations in which your communication was affected by:
   (a) Your attitude toward yourself?
   (b) Your attitude toward the subject under discussion?
   (c) The listener's attitude toward you?

4. What is meant by a process?

MATERIAL FOR THOUGHT AND DISCUSSION

We must begin by confronting the typically scientist view of the relation between science and magic. Since so many apologists of modern science, following a dialectic of simple antithesis, have looked upon magic merely as an early form of bad science, one seems to be left only with a distinction between bad science and good science. Scientific knowledge is thus presented as a terminology that gives an accurate and critically tested description of reality; and magic is presented as antithetical to such science. Hence magic is treated as an early uncritical attempt to do what science does, but under conditions where judgment and perception were impaired by the naively anthropomorphic belief that the impersonal forces of nature were motivated by personal designs. One thus confronts a flat choice between a civilized vocabulary of scientific description and a savage vocabulary of magical incantation.

In this scheme, "rhetoric" has no systematic location. . . .

Now, the basic function of rhetoric, the use of words by human agents to form attitudes or to induce actions in other human agents, is certainly not "magical." If you are in trouble, and call for help, you are no practitioner of primitive magic. You are using the primary resource of human speech in a thoroughly realistic way. Nor, on the other hand, is your utterance "science," in the strict meaning of science today, as a "semantic" or "descriptive" terminology for charting the conditions of nature from an "impersonal" point of view, regardless of one's wishes or preferences. A call for help is quite "prejudiced"; it is the most arrant kind of "wishful thinking"; it is not merely descriptive, it is *hortatory.* It is not just trying to tell how things are, in strictly "scenic" terms; it is trying to *move people.* A call for help might, of course, include purely scientific statements, or preparations for action, as a person in need might give information about particular dangers to guard against or advantages to exploit in bringing help. But the call, in itself, as such, is not scientific; it is *rhetorical.* Whereas poetical language is a kind of symbolic action, for itself and in itself, and whereas scientific [language] is a preparation for action, rhetorical language is inducement to action (or to attitude, attitude being an incipient act).

If you have only a choice between magic and science, you simply have no bin in which to accurately place such a form of expression. Hence, since "the future" is not the sort of thing one can put under a microscope, or even test by a knowledge of *exactly equivalent conditions* in the past, when you turn to political exhortation, you are involved in decisions that necessarily lie beyond the strictly scientific vocabularies of description. And since the effective politician is a "spellbinder," it seems to follow by elimination that the hortatory use of speech for political ends can be called "magic" in the discredited sense of that term.

As a result, much analysis of political exhortation comes to look simply like a survival of primitive magic, whereas it should be handled in its own terms, as an aspect of what it really is: rhetoric. . . .

To be sure, the rhetorician has the tricks of his trade. But they are not mere "bad science"; they are an "art." (*Kenneth Burke,* A Rhetoric of Motives, *pp. 41–42.*)[1]

Art is the most finished expression of truth in its myriad aspects, with the least possible obstruction in that presentation, so that those who hear or look can get most clearly and easily the thing presented. It follows that art is the highest functioning of the mind and soul of man; and it follows, too, that it requires the utmost instruction, training, and practice to become an artist of any kind.

Take music, for example: It would be a daring person who would undertake to play upon the piano or any musical instrument without having studied, not only that instrument, but the elements of music. . . .

. . . .

And so with any phase of art whatever. No sensible person would think of attempting it without information and training. For that matter shoeing a horse, driving an automobile, laying brick, keeping books, running a furrow, selling goods, and nearly everything requires knowledge and experience. Yet, curiously enough, most of us feel that we can practice without knowledge or effort the two oldest and noblest of the fine arts, writing and speaking. (*Albert J. Beveridge,* The Art of Public Speaking. *Boston: Houghton Mifflin, 1924, pp. 14–16.*)

In a world beset with sociologists, psychologists, publicists, and utopian economists, there is one product we do not lack—communications. Never before in history have so many had so much to say on such a multitude of topics to anybody who will listen.

Today everybody is communicating. We have developed the machinery to deluge the country in a turgid flow of words—written or oral—on any subject whatsoever, and to do it almost instantaneously. We possess the technology to give the people the facts, the background on the facts, and our interpretation of both the facts and their background, on any question that may arise. And we do this on a somewhat nonselective basis, regardless of whether or not the people are interested in the particular facts we are telling them about.

How much of this communication is effective is another question. Perhaps in communications, as in other things, our technology for saying things has outstripped what we have to say. Perhaps the public, accustomed to the monotonous plop, plop of bromides on its galvanized mental roof, has developed a resistance to organized communications of any kind. But if this is true, the last to discover the fact will be the communicators themselves. So absorbed are they in documenting their theories and interpreting statistics on the results of their activities that they seldom stop to think that the opinions people hold are due as much to circumstances or individual self-interest as they are to tireless efforts to advance a point of view.

This is no argument against communications. Indeed, intelligent communications is vitally needed. Nor is it intended as a case against propaganda. Obviously, a nation, a company, a union, or any other organization not only has a right but a duty to tell its story in such a way that its actions and objectives are put in a favorable light.

The intelligent communicator gives the people the facts, he interprets those facts according to the case he is presenting, he points out the answer that he wants people to come up with, and he demonstrates why it is to their advantage to do so. Furthermore, he depends on timing as much as facts to make his argument persuasive. (*James Menzies Black, "Employee Communication,"* Management Review, *July 1959, p. 4.*)

◆◆◆◆

Structurally considered, communication includes two human elements and two formal elements. The human elements are, simply stated, the communicator and the communicatee—the writer or speaker, on the one hand, and the reader or listener, on the other. Each of these human elements brings his own character, knowledge, and experience, that is, his total personality, to the act of expressing or apprehending communication. Successful transmission of meanings depends upon the force with which these human elements are brought into dynamic contact. This is equally true whether communication is limited to two persons, or, while originating with one person, it is transmitted to many.

Two formal elements constitute the essence of communication, namely, psychological and linguistic. The psychological includes all aspects of communication which incorporate human qualities into the context of expressed ideas. The sensibilities, capacities, motives, and objectives of human personality make up the psychological gist of communication. The linguistic elements, on the other hand, are intrinsic to language regarded as verbal entities and verbal structures.

In theory, these diverse elements, psychological and linguistic, may be separated and distinguished for purposes of analysis, study, and discussion. In real communication, however, they are totally fused. Once spoken or written, a communication is inseminated with a semantic power exceeding the verbal units or arrangements into which it is structured. A theorist who aims at improved communication in business and industry must recognize both the distinctness and the unity of the two elements, psychological and linguistic. While content of the words is psychological, their verbal structure is graphic or sonic. The proportion of purely linguistic or purely psychological meaning in a statement is difficult to determine because the two component elements are fused in the actual statement. None the less, some observations may be made about the two elements, distinctly conceptualized, in considering training objectives and methods:

Psychologically, better communication requires training for the communicator in: (a) recognizing the real character of the subject matter under discussion; (b) eliminating bias, prejudice, and other distortions; (c) structuring ideas according to norms of completeness, clarity, and coherence; (d) critically evaluating the structured ideas; (e) psychological synthesizing of subject matter, point of view, purpose, and method; (f) most importantly, understanding the inter- and intra-personal aspects of communication.

Linguistically, better communication demands training in: (a) delimitation of word meanings and distinction between denotations and connotations; (b) economical verbal statements, oral and written; (c) more particularizing and less generalizing; (d) more emphasis on content and less on formality in expression; (e) fuller understanding of style differentiations, such as learned, plain; formal, informal; technical, general; (f) more assiduous attention to individual differences in semantic capacity in inter-personal communication.

In sum, psychologically improved communication requires first of all a fuller awareness by business management of the psychological content of verbal statement. Conversely, linguistic improvement demands a fuller awareness of the semantic implications of words and word structures. (*Richard Sexton and Virginia Staudt, "The Communications Clinic Approach,"* Journal of General Psychology, *January 1959, pp. 59–60.*)

3

He that has sense knows that learning is not knowledge, but the art of using it.—Steele

CHANGING BELIEFS AND GAINING ACCEPTANCE

Most speaking is persuasive in its purpose. Sometimes we attempt to cause the listener to form an opinion or accept an idea that he did not have before. On other occasions we attempt to change his point of view. But some kind of persuasion is necessary if we are to motivate the listener to take a certain action. Some understanding of one way in which persuasion can take place is important if we are to understand the communication process fully.

Many, many stimuli are impinging upon us all the time. As you read, the words on this page form one stimulus; you are also more or less aware of the actions of a roommate, the music of a radio, voices in the hall, the heat of the room, a state of hunger or drowsiness, and many other stimuli. Any individual will perceive at a given time only a limited number of the stimuli present. You may not realize that your roommate is present, or the radio turned on. You may be hungry, but not hungry enough to block your reading or understanding. You may seem to be concentrating on reading, while in reality you are attempting to overhear a conversation taking place in the hall. From all the stimuli present, you are choosing those to which you will pay attention at any given time.

The oral communication situation presents similar problems. Yesterday you heard a professor talk for approximately an hour. There were many stimuli present. Can you remember any details as to how he was dressed, or how he used his voice, or what physical movements he made? What details do you remember about the other students in the room? How many were present? How did they respond to the lecture? What about the physical aspects of the room? Were the windows up or down, how many windows and doors were there, and how comfortable was the temperature? What extraneous noises could be heard? What was your own physical and mental state? What did the speaker have to say? What were his important ideas and how did he develop them? You may remember a great deal about the girl in front of you, the heat of the room, and the best joke in the lecture, but little of what the speaker wanted you to hear. Or you may remember a considerable amount of the lecture content but little about the physical aspects of the surroundings. Hundreds of stimuli were present, but you perceived only a few. And the perception of your classmates in the room was probably quite different from yours. During a dormitory bull session—to consider an informal context—stimuli are coming from a nearby card game, the hi-fi, others in the session, your feeling that you should be studying, frustration over a poor exam written earlier that day, and anticipation of a return phone call concerning a weekend date, as well as from the person who is speaking at the moment. Various stimuli, some conducive to good communication and some not, are present over coffee, at a committee meeting, and in all other communication situations.

It is evident, then, that the speaker must make a conscious effort to have the listener perceive as many as possible of the stimuli that the speaker considers desirable and to reduce conflicting stimuli. The primary methods of achieving this goal are good organization, interesting and meaningful supporting material, and fluent and forceful delivery. These techniques are important not in themselves but as means by which the listener can be led to concentrate on desirable stimuli.

In the learning process, the perception of stimuli is followed by the decoding of the stimuli perceived. For example, there may be smoke in a room. You may or may not perceive it; if you do, you may identify what type of smoke it is. It may be cigarette smoke, or wood smoke, or smoke from a chemical reaction. Such interpretation of stimuli perceived is called "decoding."

During communication through words, the decoding process must also take place. For example, in a discussion of study habits various participants use such phrases as "study hours," "undisturbed conditions," "low comprehension," and "inability to integrate." Some of the listeners translate these words into their own language, substituting "reading time" for "study hours," "no noise" for "undisturbed conditions," "don't understand" for "low comprehension," and "can't think" for "inability to integrate." The danger is that even at this level the translations may not mean exactly what the speaker had in mind. Decoding in oral communication can be even more complicated. Sometimes a listener has to decode a whole sentence or idea by putting it into words that he can understand. The statement, "The only time a stimulus-response relationship is altered is when the organism interprets the existing relationship as less rewarding than a possible alternative relationship," may have no meaning to the listener, until it is translated to, "The only way a habit can be changed is by offering something more rewarding."

The understanding that results from the decoding process will depend on the circumstances and on the past experiences of the listener. For instance, if you identify the smoke that you smell as wood smoke and there is a fireplace in the room, you will decode the stimulus in one way. But if you identify the smoke as wood smoke and there is no fireplace in the room, you will make quite a different interpretation. In the discussion of study habits, the words "undisturbed conditions" may mean utter quiet to one person whereas another would interpret the words as meaning no disturbance above the normal level of dormitory noise.

The speaker's goal, so far, is to stir up in the mind of the listener a meaning or understanding that is as close as possible to his own. Awareness of the complications of the listener's problem can be helpful here. If the listener finds the interpretive process too difficult he might refuse to make the effort to listen effectively. This would be true, for example, if technical words outside of his experience were used. Or the words themselves might be familiar to the listener but the concept so new or so complex that it seems to require too much effort to understand. In these circumstances, communication is bound to fail because the listener's experience has not equipped him to decode and interpret the speaker's words except with more than normal effort. The speaker must know as much about his listener as possible so that his language will be familiar and his approach can be easily followed. Knowledge of the listener will also help the speaker to determine how fast or how slowly he must unravel the thoughts that he is presenting. Some listeners can decode certain thoughts quickly while others need more time and more detail. The study of the listener in Chapter 5 will assist you in analyzing the individuals to whom you speak so that the decoding process will be as easy as possible.

Simply evoking meaning is not enough, however, when we are asking listeners to accept an idea, to change a belief or attitude, or to take some action. The speaker must go further and encourage the listener to make some specific response. The possible responses are many, but a few examples will help to clarify the point we are making.

One response that might be sought is to get the listener to ask himself certain questions about his beliefs and attitudes: Why do I feel that a liberal arts background is so important for me? Why do I feel that I must receive professional training while in college? Am I free of racial prejudice or do I just give lip-service to lack of prejudice because I seldom have contact with racial minorities? How do I really study? Are extracurricular activities really important, and if so, why?

A second type of response is acceptance of the idea being presented. Examples might be: Nonconformity is not always expressed by bizarre behavior; nonviolent methods are not always the most effective way to secure civil rights for minorities; under proper controls, television can be an effective method of teaching in a classroom; graduate work is becoming almost a necessity in most business fields today.

Another kind of response is achieved when the listener makes a commitment to himself to take some action when the appropriate situation presents itself. Possible responses here might be: I will bring the matter of study conditions up at the next house meeting; I will register for a philosophy of religion course next semester; I will join the Thursday evening group that helps tutor underprivileged children.

REWARD

Two mistakes concerning the desired response are often made in communication. The first is to talk about a topic in such general terms that the listener cannot understand what response is sought. The second is to assume that if the listener understands he will automatically respond with belief and action. Let us discuss the second of these errors in detail. We might understand the evils of cigarette smoking but not stop smoking. We might agree when someone tells us that our foreign policy needs reshaping but think no more about it. We might understand that our study habits are not the best but make no changes for the better. The speaker, therefore, must not only achieve understanding; he must strive for a type of acceptance that eventually will have an effect. He must evoke in the listener a response that will be meaningful and make the communication worthwhile. To do this, he must make clear to the listener what will happen as a consequence of the response sought. We are mainly interested in how things affect us, and as a result of this self-interest we seldom feel strongly about matters that seem to have little relationship to us as individuals. Since we tend to believe and act on ideas that give us satisfaction and to avoid things that hurt us or that we consider undesirable, any discussion of consequence must introduce the concept of reward and punishment. Research studies generally indicate that the promise of reward has a more lasting effect on us than the threat of punishment, but fear of the latter may be useful in certain situations.

Suppose that you wish to persuade someone to give up cigarettes, to study differently, to join a peace group, to agree with you concerning censorship, to vote for a certain candidate, to approach automation with a certain attitude, or to see the need for farm subsidies. On all of these topics, and hundreds of similar ones, you are attempting to get the listener to make a response. Certain questions need to be answered satisfactorily to make this response a real possibility: (1) What reward are you offering that particular individual? (2) Does this reward affect that individual enough to get him intellectually and emotionally involved with the topic? (3) Is the effort he must *personally* put forth too great, in terms of the reward offered, to get him to change his attitude, his belief, or his action? (4) How soon can he expect the reward?

Reward for the individual

One of the errors commonly made in communication is to fail to identify clearly the possible reward for the listener or listeners. Possible rewards that seem obvious to the speaker may not enter the mind of the listener at all. Suppose you plan to ask your fellow students to support a movement to raise the activities fee one dollar a semester. You and a few other students may recognize the vital need for more money, but your listeners may not. If you merely point out that more activities could be sponsored if the group had more money available, the communication could well fail. You must point out how the individuals in that group specifically might benefit from the increase in funds. If a listener feels that the money will be spent on more and better social events and he is not a socially minded person, he will not support the change. However, if he has literary interests and you point out that a portion of the increase will go toward better campus publications, you will be more effective. It is important that the rewards be discussed specifically and that they be tied to the interests of the listeners to whom you are speaking.

Involving the listener

Not all people are motivated to the same degree by the same things. Some people respond to such rewards as "justice," "the rights of the individual," and "better education." These rewards leave other individuals cold, or at least do not motivate them strongly. Some individuals are highly motivated by such ideas as "increasing your income," "getting ahead," or "attaining a better position." In contrast, however, these rewards have little or no motivation for some people, and a few will even argue against them as worthy goals. If the reactions of individuals were as predictable as those of chemicals, the behavorial sciences would be simpler, but perhaps duller. Different people react differently, and the same individual reacts differently at various times and under varying conditions. This makes life more interesting, but it makes the communication problem more complicated.

Recently, two people in the same class discussed the cigarette problem. One pointed out that non-smokers live a few years longer than smokers, and that smoking increases tendencies toward disease, particularly heart disease. The group was composed of students 18 and 19 years of age, and the response was generally weak. The other student pointed out what happens to the human system when one smokes. Some dramatic visual material and demonstrations made clear what happens *now* to the smoker. This speaker also pointed out the cost of cigarettes over a 20-year period, emphasizing what the savings could mean to individuals in the group. These rewards and punishments involved the listeners to a much greater degree than those presented in the first speech, and the responses that resulted were much stronger. No one argued that the first speaker was misrepresenting the facts, but they pointed out that they could not at their ages get very much interested in the threat of a heart attack at 50 or 55, or in the possibility of adding a few years to their lives some 50 or 60 years from now.

The same holds true for other topics. Automation may bring lower cost per product or greater unemployment, but the listener needs to know how this reward or punishment will affect him. Peace is fine, but what can one individual do about it? Censorship may be bad or necessary, but am I not able to choose my own reading material? Television commercials may be silly, misleading, or too frequent, but so what? Just don't pay any attention to them! To combat the attitudes in these and similar reactions, the speaker must go as far as possible in showing what *that* listener stands to gain or lose if the communication is to get the listener to make the desired response.

Effort required for the reward

All students would like to improve their study habits, but how many are willing to put forth the effort required to follow a new method? If a speaker is to be successful in getting the desired response on this subject from the average listener, the reward must appear great enough in the mind of the listener to make worthwile the effort involved in changing the habit. If the new method means a minor change in procedure with no additional time involved, a simple reward may be satisfactory. If, however, the new study method requires the purchase and reading of a book, additional time to master new techniques, and more effort during study periods, the reward for many students would have to be both certain and substantial. The student who is about to flunk out of school, or who at his present achievement rate will not graduate, or to whom graduate school will be closed unless he makes higher grades may be motivated to make the effort necessary under the new method. But the average student who is "getting by" and generally meeting his own educational standards may not have a strong enough desire to improve his grades to make the effort required by the new method.

Thus the speaker must not only clearly identify the consequences for the listener and be sure that those consequences involve him, but the reward must appear to the listener to be worth the effort involved. Most individuals want their church to continue its activities, and want their club or organization to thrive, want justice for all people, want good schools and teachers, and want many other things that are "good." But how much effort will they invest to achieve these goals? For most, the effort will be minimal unless the reward is great enough to motivate them.

At times the speaker may need to limit the response he seeks in a given communication because of the effort required. If the whole action he seeks might look quite involved, he may seek a more modest response at first, hoping that after the listener has achieved a limited goal with a limited effort, the opportunity for expansion of the response may come at a later date. As we have pointed out, communication is a continuing process and most communication is not limited to a one-time occasion.

Immanence of the reward

The new study method discussed above may influence some listeners to change their habits for a time. They see the value of the new method and begin to try it out. We must consider, however, how long they will keep up the new effort if no obvious reward is in sight. Let us suppose that one has to wait a full semester before the results are seen. To follow a new and strenuous pattern for three or four months, not knowing what effect the change will have, is a lot to ask. Many people follow a set of physical exercises for a few days, but when the waistline is not immediately smaller or biceps larger, other things begin to get in the way of the activity. Cigarette sales charts show that many people stopped smoking for a short time immediately after the publication of the Surgeon-General's report, but they later returned to their previous habit. College students typically start each year with a sincere desire to "do better," but the motivation often does not hold very long.

Thus, when possible, it is helpful for the speaker to point

out short-term rewards or measurement of rewards when the total effect will be a long time in coming. For instance, the long-term reward for a new study method may be better grades at the end of a semester, but the speaker can point out that certain self-administered tests, the making of daily outlines, or even class quizzes will show the listener that the new method is having good results. These short-term results may help to sustain motivation until the real goal is accomplished.

IMBALANCE AND PERSUASION

As long as any individual feels that his present beliefs, attitudes, and actions are bringing him satisfactory results, he will continue them. Thus, if we are to effect changes, we must make the listener feel that his present ways are not wholly adequate and that new methods will increase his satisfaction. The speaker must show that new beliefs, attitudes, and actions will bring the listener greater rewards or fewer punishments than he is receiving at present. Merely pointing out some evil or making a new pattern understood is not sufficient. The new response must create in the listener an imbalance, a desire for something more rewarding.

What is a satisfactory reward? Basically any reward that better meets the needs, wants, and desires of a particular individual is enough to get him to respond. The reward offered need not be earth-shaking or revolutionary—a guaranteed life income or appointment to a cabinet-level post. The aiding of a worthwhile cause, satisfying one's curiosity, becoming a member of a group, and many similar rewards are often effective. It is important that the reward be made meaningful to the listener and that it be a reward to which he can respond. Successful communication is geared to the people present.

CONCLUSION

The effective communicator is conscious of the process by which change takes place. He recognizes that while he is talking, many stimuli are bombarding the listener. Unless the listener perceives as many as possible of the stimuli that carry the speaker's message, the chances of successful communication are limited.

After perception, the listener must decode the stimuli and attach the proper meaning to them. The speaker can help by consciously approaching each step with the listener in mind. The listener can think only in his own terms, about his own experiences based on his own background. The speaker must be conscious of the listener's background, experience, and language facility.

Clear understanding alone, however, does not always lead to persuasion. The speaker must show the effects of a desired change on the listener by pointing out the rewards involved and showing their value to the listener. The effort necessary to reap the rewards and the time factor involved must also be taken into consideration.

Since each listener is an individual with his own needs, wants, and desires, all the material used to persuade must be adapted to the listener to create some dissatisfaction with his present situation and offer the rewards of the new.

REVIEW QUESTIONS

1. What steps must a listener go through before he finally responds to a communication?
2. What do we mean by "reward" in communication?
3. In each of the following examples, is the reward likely to be suitable to the listener(s)? Why?
   (a) A social chairman invites one of his instructors to chaperone a party.
   (b) A fraternity man invites some acquaintances who happen to be passing by to help build a float for homecoming.
   (c) A student in a speech class asks his hearers to write to their congressmen in favor of support for the United Nations.
   (d) At a party, someone asks for a volunteer to pick a card—any card.

(e) A member of the golf team tries to persuade a friend to take up golf because it is a game that can be played right on through his life after college, and even after retirement.

4. How does a speaker create an imbalance in the minds of his hearers?

PROJECTS

1. Choose a problem on which there is a difference of opinion between students and the administration at your institution. How might the two groups decode different meanings from a discussion in which both were represented?

2. Determine how your best friend's experience has led him to attach certain meanings to such words as:
   (a) liberal education
   (b) love
   (c) military service
   (d) stock market
   (e) missiles
   Has your experience led you to attach different meanings?

3. Can you recall situations in which you agreed with the action sought by someone communicating with you, but the reward was not great enough for you to change your action? What rewards would have made you change, if any?

4. Analyze the lectures of one of your professors. What rewards do you think he had in mind for you as he prepared the lecture? What rewards did he actually offer? What rewards did you expect from the lecture?

5. Psychologists tell us that a person will do anything suggested to him unless there is a reason for not doing it. Analyze this statement in the light of the discussion of rewards in the text.

MATERIAL FOR THOUGHT AND DISCUSSION

Of eloquence, in particular, it is the more necessary to ascertain the proper notion, because there is not anything concerning which false notions have been more prevalent. Hence, it has been so often, and is still at this day, in disrepute with many. When you speak to a plain man of eloquence, or in praise of it, he is apt to hear you with very little attention. He conceives eloquence to signify a certain trick of speech; the art of varnishing weak arguments plausibly; or of speaking so as to please and tickle the ear. "Give me good sense," says he, "and keep your eloquence for boys." He is in the right, if eloquence were what he conceives it to be. It would be then a very contemptible art, indeed, below the study of any wise or good man. But nothing can be more remote from the truth. To be truly eloquent, is to speak to the purpose. For the best definition, which, I think, can be given of eloquence, is the art of speaking in such a manner as to attain the end for which we speak. (*Hugh Blair,* Lectures on Rhetoric and Belles Lettres. *Philadelphia: Matthew Carey, 1793, Vol. I, pp. 459–460.*)

It is thus apparent that a person's decision is influenced by previously received communications from two categories of sources—those external to the organism and those internal to it (and the latter includes memory, conditioned responses, glandular state, and so on). Likewise it appears that all communications are generated by previous communications—or, more precisely, by a combination of them. A person decides as a result of the receipt of information about the external situation, and from within him, such as goals, plans, attitudes, drives, and so forth. And the communications which he transmits generate further communication in and from those who perceive them. A decision can thus be regarded as a point in time when one or a number of communications are combined to become one or a number of different communications. It is important to note that many may generate one or a few, and one or a few may generate many. (*John T. Dorsey, "A Communication Model for Administration,"* Administrative Science Quarterly, *December 1957, p. 310.*)

The existential situation is the actual, present set of conditions in which the speaker utters what he has to say. It is made up of three parts: (1) the total expressiveness of the bodily presence and personality of the speaker; (2) the total responsiveness of the bodily presence and personality of the listener or listeners; (3) the events leading to the present from which arise the alternative courses of action determining the good and evil in the lives of those involved.

The kind of speech which communicates the sense of good and evil most effectively is here called "creative interchange" to distinguish it from other forms of speech. By creative interchange we mean that kind of communication which does three things: (1) creates an understanding in the listener of the viewpoint of the speaker; (2) integrates this viewpoint into the perspective of the listener so that he has a more comprehensive understanding; (3) communicates the sense of good and evil so that each can be aware of the way the other values the alternative possibilities arising out of the situation. . . .

All thought, all striving, all knowledge, all action, all decision, indeed the whole of human life is directed and controlled by what men judge to be good and evil. Therefore, the all-important part of any communication is the view of good and evil involved in it. Logic, information, evidence, knowledge, and rationality take on great value when they serve to communicate a profound sense of good and evil and clarify the distinctions between them. But when information, technique, and rational order are not put to communicating this profound intuition, or when they are treated as ends in themselves, they become trivial in the sense that they make no appreciable difference in the conduct of human living. Nothing can make an appreciable difference in human life unless it motivates thought, feeling and action. Since the sense of good and evil alone can motivate, all knowledge and all forms of reason are trivial unless they carry with them this driving sense. . . .

Speech, both as a field for research and as a practicing art, carries a special moral responsibility for promoting the kind of communication which expands the range of what men can appreciate as good and distinguish as evil. If creative interchange is not the best name to distinguish this kind of speech, some other name can be devised. The name is not important, but this kind of communication is, since all distinctively human values are created by creative interchange, beginning with early infancy and continuing throughout the life of the individual. If creative interchange does not occur effectively between parent and child, the child becomes neurotic or psychotic or otherwise unfit to live with other human beings in ways of mutual trust and mutual support. (*Henry W. Wieman, "Speech in the Existential Situation,"* Quarterly Journal of Speech, *April 1961, pp. 150–151, 153.*)

The teacher's comments occur in a group setting, and can be heard by the entire class. When the teacher gives a feedback with high information, it is immediately clear to the class whether the student's response was correct and, if not, how far it deviated from being correct. Individuals who consistently receive comments indicating that they know the material are intelligent, understand the implication of complicated points, etc., and might achieve a relatively high social status within the class—while those consistently receiving information labelling their responses as faulty might receive a lower-status evaluation. This would not be possible if everyone in the class did not have the chance to hear the assessments received by everyone else, and to compare those received by themselves with those received by others.

The fact that feedback occurs in a group setting indicates that no matter to whom it is directed (and it may be directed toward a single student, a group of students, or the total class), it has a potential effect on the entire class. Students who are not actively participating in a class discussion, but who are following carefully, can vicariously participate in the questions, responses, and feedbacks given to other students, and be affected by them somewhat similarly to those which they receive more directly. In fact, assuming that most teacher commentary is directed toward individual students, it seems quite likely that, at any single time, a large part of the effective feedback is of this vicarious or indirect type. It is doubtful whether a reinforcement attached to a vicarious feedback would have as great an effect as one received directly by the student; on the other hand, the greater detachment and lack of direct involvement may enhance the student's opportunity to follow the total development of a discussion. Students may be encouraged to undertake roles of certain types if they see the relevant behavior rewarded in other students. (*Daniel Solomon and Larry Rosenberg, "Teacher-Student Feedback and Classroom Social Structure,"* Journal of Social Psychology, *April 1964, p. 202.*)

The commercialization of mass communication has led to a depersonalization of human relations and to a glorification of clichés and slogans. The standardized response begins more and more to substitute for deeply felt, personalized expression, and—as a perhaps last defense—the human ear has adapted itself to sort and disregard a considerable number of verbal messages that emerge from radio loudspeakers and television sets, just as it formerly accommodated itself to the task of absorbing what was being said. This trend goes even further. As mass communication increasingly tends toward sloganizing and the use of proven formulas, literature tends toward journalism, reversing a trend of two hundred years during which journalism aspired to the condition of literature. Many book publishers frankly admit that they have become less and less adventurous and chance-taking in matters of editorial policy, looking most searchingly for best sellers to relax the economic squeeze in which they are caught, or relying on instructional and inspirational "how to do it" books, in which everything is reduced to a recipe or device that is simple and can be quickly acquired by everyone. When the "how to" is violently disjoined from the "what"—one of the major trends of popular thinking today—communication is regarded as merely a peripheral skill unrelated to the core of personality and to all those thoughts and feelings that formerly characterized an individual human being.

This trend is also responsible for shaping hollow and unreal face-to-face encounters that in even the recent past would have been considered not only unethical but definitely pathological. Today's salesmen, for example, are trained to turn on a line, to envisage for the customer a sense of prestige and success that attends the purchase of an expensive car that the customer may not be able to afford, or to create feelings of emergency and fear when grooming and personal hygiene are involved. The line between fantasy and reality becomes increasingly blurred, and the individual is given less and less of a chance to live in an environment where honest and well-meant advice is obtainable. The upsurge of psychiatric treatment is thus not unrelated to these developments, as more and more people have come to feel that they are lost in an unreal world and want to find themselves.

Present-day thinking has created a verbal unreality. Primarily in middle-class circles—particularly among many administrators, executives, almost all politicians, and even doctors and lawyers—

words tend to be treated as absolutes. The fact that words are sounds referring to ideas or events is frequently overlooked altogether; in the act of speaking or writing, words are invested, in their minds, with substance and body, so that words become things in themselves. Then too, the assumption is often made that words are the only means of communication, whereas commonplace silent actions are not interpreted as having communicative value.

The Machiavellian use of communication for deception and control has been employed for centuries, but the commercialization of communication in business and politics is a fairly recent development. These new techniques not only employ deception about products—a device merchants have always worked—but have introduced a radically new idea: to delude the individual about his own personal attitudes toward other people and things. This approach in effect undermines his ethical and moral sense, and destroys his trust in his fellow men. Against these recent developments, few defensive measures have yet developed. However, a countertrend is apparent. As educators and religious and civic leaders have become alarmed at the trend of events, a growing intellectual and scientific consciousness about communications as a problem has developed. In certain literary circles, among those who deal with language and semantics—and increasingly among some psychiatrists—there is a deepening regard for problems of meaning and a concern with the individualistic and idiosyncratic attributes of words as opposed to their dictionary definitions. Cybernetics engineers and biologists have dealt with the communication networks and feedback patterns; psychiatrists, cultural anthropologists, and social workers have studied problems of social action and interpersonal and group relations.

The trend of a number of these approaches has been toward an essential concern with nonverbal forms of communication and with the verbal form largely in its pragmatic aspects. Such a reaction against the overevaluation of the spoken and printed word, and against both commercialism and the relative exclusion of nonverbal elements, can in one sense be interpreted as a move toward safety. In a time of political or ideological crisis, there exists a tendency to censor words in the naive belief that thought can be brought under absolute control. Although books can be burned, the use of certain words legally outlawed, and even the act of listening to particular broadcasts or speeches marked as a criminal offense, communication through silent action is more difficult to suppress. It has been widely noted how, under authoritatian regimes, human beings turn more and more toward the perception of the nonverbal, the evaluation of nonverbally codified things, and expression through gesture and action. . . .

When communicating with each other, people not only exchange messages containing information that refers to outside events, but they also exchange messages referring to the communication process itself. These metacommunicative messages include:

The specific instructions given by a sender about the way messages ought to be interpreted and the respective interpretations made by the receiver.

Implicit instructions contained in what is commonly referred to as role.

Institutionalized instructions, either explicit or implicit, that are inherent in the structure of social situations and the rules governing the flow of messages.

When a person has expressed an idea in words to others, a reaction is necessarily expected. And this reaction contributes to clarify, extend, or alter the original idea. Feedback, therefore, refers to the process of correction through incorporation of information about effects achieved. When a person perceives the results produced by his own actions, the information so derived will influence subsequent actions. Feedback of information thus becomes a steering device upon which learning and the correction of errors and misunderstandings are based. . . . (*Jurgen Ruesch and Weldon Kees,* Nonverbal Communication: Notes on the Visual Perception of Human Relations. *Berkeley: University of California Press, 1961, pp. 4–5, 7.*)

4

We know accurately only when we know little; with knowledge doubt increases.—Goethe

FIRST STEPS IN PREPARING TO COMMUNICATE

The importance of knowledge in successful communication has already been discussed in the first chapter of this book: knowledge leads to good ideas, and good ideas are the basis of successful communication. A common mistake, however, is to assume that any information that is known is ready for communication. The fact that a person has read some source of information, had an experience, or heard someone talk about a certain subject does not mean that he is ready to formulate an opinion and communicate it to others. There are several intervening steps between collecting these bits of information and being ready to communicate. These steps are the subject of this chapter.

Our experience, our reading, and our contact with others have given us a smattering of information on many things. Some of these topics have affected us enough so that we have developed a real interest in them. This interest and the few bits of information can trap us into jumping to unsound conclusions that we may then communicate to others. This is a serious error. Before we have the right to communicate, we must take three steps: (1) we must become aware of what we know *and what we do not know;* (2) we must analyze our knowledge to see what, if any, conclusions we may draw; and (3) we must decide whether we need to gather more information, either to correct or strengthen our conclusions or to make the ideas clear and meaningful to our listeners.

The time required to complete these steps may vary from seconds to days. If a quick analysis of our knowledge convinces us that we have the necessary information to draw conclusions and support them, we are ready to communicate. If, however, our analysis shows gaps in our information so that our conclusions will be weak or our support inadequate, we must spend whatever time is necessary to overcome these weaknesses.

Failure to follow these steps can be very damaging to the effectiveness of our communication. Success with the uninformed and the unthinking requires no study since even weak communication may be successful if the listeners are as ignorant on the topic as the speaker. However, if the listeners are knowledgeable, or perceptive enough to request further support, or alert enough to ask penetrating questions, a lack of adequate study of the topic soon becomes apparent.

This all sounds very well, you may say, for the formal speaking situation, when you know some time in advance that you are to give a speech on a specific topic; but for the more common communication situations in which we find ourselves, all this preparation is simply not possible. If you give the matter a little further thought, you will discover that preparation is possible in more situations than you at first might expect. PTA members know in advance when the budget is to be acted upon; members of the committee for the spring prom know that one of their tasks will be to find a suitable place to hold the dance; student senators know that some recommendations concerning graduation requirements are to be debated at the next meeting; you know when you are going to bring a matter up for discussion in a house meeting. In all of these situations, those who will be taking part in the discussion have the opportunity to prepare themselves in advance. When the participants are not prepared, discussions of such topics are frequently unsatisfactory.

From time to time, a topic may come up unexpectedly in a group in which you find yourself participating, and it may become apparent that the members do not have the information necessary to make a reasonable decision. You should point this fact out. If the topic is of importance, and the other members are conscientious, they will then make arrangements to get the information. On those few occasions when circumstances may require an immediate decision and adequate information on which to take action wisely is not available, it is important that the group recognize the fact that it is acting on the basis of insufficient knowledge.

SOURCES OF INFORMATION

There are three main sources of material available to a communicator: (1) the information he brings from the past, (2) further reading, and (3) additional listening.

Our own knowledge

Our past experience, including our reading and contact with others, has provided us with a good deal of information concerning a variety of subjects. We may mishandle this information in two ways: (1) we may fail to attach any real meaning to what we know; or (2) we may fail to recognize the limitations our inadequate knowledge places on us.

Our background in a limited number of areas may be complete enough so that we can draw valid conclusions and be ready for communication. Our personal experiences in a given area may be rather extensive: we may have held a variety of summer jobs; we may have lived in a foreign country for some period; our hobby may have given us a good background in astronomy or electronics. Our reading and listening may have built up a background of knowledge in certain areas of interest.

This is not the usual pattern, however. Our experience in a given area is usually quite restricted, our reading limited to a few sources, and we may have listened to only a few individuals, some of whom may not have been well informed on the subject. Recognition of these limitations is essential to a good communicator.

It is equally important that we attach meaning to our experiences, our reading, and our listening—that we recognize their significance and learn from them. Mere participation is valueless unless we attach meaning to the experience. A school administrator was once chided because he had hired a young applicant rather than one who had been teaching for 20 years. He answered, "She hasn't 20 years of experience, but one experience 20 times." A student who has been involved in student government for two years will have no worthwhile ideas on the subject unless he has tried to analyze the meaning of the experience—to learn something from it. The same holds true for reading and listening. Many people spend considerable time in either or both of these activities without discovering any new ideas.

In spite of the fact that our knowledge in most of the fields about which we talk is based upon limited and casual experience, reading, and listening, it is this largely undigested store of information upon which we commonly draw when we find it necessary to communicate with others. We discuss complicated problems of politics and religion, to name two topics popular with most college students, without having made a very thorough study of our own beliefs; our understanding of the beliefs of others, and their reasons for holding such beliefs, is commonly negligible.

Thus, the first step in preparing to communicate is to take stock of your present level of knowledge on a topic and analyze its meaning. Occasionally when you have completed this step you will be ready for communication. More often you will merely have formed the basis for further study.

Knowledge from further reading

A student gains some interest in and information about the use of intelligence tests in a psychology class. A businessman recognizes some danger signals in figures showing an increase in overtime pay for his employees. A socially minded person has seen and heard some things concerning reduction of cavities in children's teeth through the use of fluorides.

The student knows that the subject of intelligence tests is likely to come up for discussion in his contacts with fellow students. The businessman knows that he must take steps to change the situation, and that eventually he will have to tell someone what needs to be done. Fluoridation becomes a lively issue in the community. None of the three individuals mentioned may have any intention of making a formal speech on the topic, but each probably will want to make his opinions felt when the occasion presents itself. And all of them, after analyzing present knowledge, will probably decide that they do not have the information necessary to influence others through communication.

One method by which all of these individuals can increase their knowledge is by reading. The student may use the library. The businessman may read reports from his own or similar businesses, look over one or more of the many books written for management personnel to see what is said on the matter, or request a special report on the problem and read the results. The socially conscious person may read pamphlets published by health groups, dental associations, and organizations for and against fluoridation. The variations in sources are many and will depend on the communicator, the possible listeners, the topic, and the depth of information needed. The important point is that, after interest in an idea has been developed, any person should examine the sources available to him to be sure that his background is adequate before he even thinks of communicating to someone on the subject.

Since the library is a prime source of reading materials, let us examine some of the more basic procedures to be followed in using it. The potential of a library depends on its size and selectivity of material, but there are five main sources of bibliographical information: the card catalog, the periodical indices, newspaper indices, special reference books, and government documents.

Card catalog. The card catalog contains basic information concerning the books that are available in a particular library. Books may be used, of course, at various stages of preparation, but they are particularly important in building an adequate background so that an individual will see the whole topic, not just a limited phase of it. Books can help the communicator to ask himself the proper questions on which to base additional study of the subject. The method of filing cards in the catalog may vary from library to library, but cards are generally available under at least two headings: author and subject matter. Your previous knowledge of a subject may include the names of men who have written about the topic. In this case, the author listing will be of help. If you are not familiar with the names of authorities in the field, the general subject headings in the card catalog will list the books available on the topic. For instance, if you are looking for material on speech or communication, you might go to both of these headings. Cards under these general headings may refer you to other subject titles for books pertaining to speech. In one library, for instance, the cross-reference under "Motivation" refers the reader to "Psychology—Motivation," "Marketing—Motivation Research," and "Employee—Motivation."

The following reproduction of a book entry in the card catalog shows what information is available on a typical card. The book was published in the U.S. It was issued by a university press, and so the information included will probably be quite scholarly and may be highly technical. The card also gives the number of pages, and tells you that illustrations and bibliographies are included. Some cards even list the table of contents. The cross-references at the bottom of the card suggest other headings under which you might look for similar books.

400

C424 **Cherry, Colin.**

On human communication; a review, a survey, and a criticism. [Cambridge] Technology Press of Massachusetts Institute of Technology [1957]

333 p. illus. 24 cm. (Studies in communication)

Includes bibliographies.

1. Communication. 2. Language and languages. I. Title.

P90.C55 400 56—9820 ‡

Library of Congress [57i2 10]

Periodical indices. The most efficient way of finding the articles that have been published in magazines on a given subject is to use the various periodical indices. Most of you are probably familiar with *The Reader's Guide to Periodical Literature,* which indexes the contents of the more popular magazines of general interest. But you should not stop here. In preparing for communication, you should also consult the *International Index,* if available. This index includes more scholarly magazines than *The Reader's Guide,* and therefore the information found there is likely to be more authoritative than that found in popular magazines. Almost all of the magazines in the *International Index* are printed in English.

Other indices may be of real value, depending on your subject. The *Business Index* contains a listing of articles in leading business and industrial periodicals. Articles concerned with education and with research in that area are listed in the *Education Index.* The *Agricultural Index,* the *Art Index,* and the *Music Index* contain listings of periodical articles in each of these fields. The *Public Affairs Information Service* indexes books, periodicals, pamphlets, and public documents concerning the fields of government, sociology, and business.

This list by no means includes all of the specialized indices available, but it will give the reader a starting point for the use of this type of bibliographical aid.

Many indices list material by author and title, but the subject matter headings will probably be of most value to the reader. Many of these headings are subdivided. For instance, the main topic "Communication" may be divided into articles concerning speech and writing, religion, social aspects of communication, and communication in management, medicine, science, the military, research, for the police, and with workers. The main and subheadings will give the reader an efficient method of finding the articles of most value to him. The titles of the various articles under each heading will give the reader some idea of what the articles are about. An entry will list the volume number, the date, and the page numbers so that the reader can find the issue of the magazine for perusal if an article seems pertinent. Recent issues of magazines may not yet be bound and can usually be found in the periodical room of the library.

Newspaper indices. The *New York Times Index* will perform the same task for the reader in the newspaper field that the periodical indices do for magazine articles. This index, again alphabetized under subject headings, refers the reader to the proper date, page, and column for newspaper items in which he may have an interest. The date for an item located in the *Times Index* may lead the reader to issues of other newspapers of the same date if the topic was of contemporary interest.

Reference books. The fourth important source for the reader is reference books. For general knowledge, the reader may wish to go to one of the encyclopedias such as the *Encyclopaedia Britannica* or the *Encyclopedia Americana.* For more specialized coverage, encyclopedias are available in such fields as the social sciences, banking and finance, world history, and religion and ethics.

Specific facts, particularly statistics, can be found in such reference books as the *Statistical Abstract,* the *World Almanac,* and the *Information Please Almanac.*

Government documents. Agencies of all levels of government—local, state, national, and international—are continually issuing studies, reports, and other official papers. Various indices are available to publications of, for instance, the United Nations or the U.S. government. Because of the variety and volume of these materials, most libraries have special librarians in charge of documents. If the reader has never used government publications before, he would do well to begin by asking the assistance of the documents librarian.

Many libraries have specialized resources in addition to those mentioned here. The five major groups of source materials discussed above are found in almost all sizable libraries.

The handling of material gleaned from your study of these sources is just as important as finding the sources. When you find a book or article that looks useful, you should skim the material. Many of the sources located can be eliminated quickly because their content is not pertinent to your approach to the subject. They may be too general or too technical for your understanding. This quick skimming will help you evaluate the usefulness of the remaining material: it may furnish good background, or lend itself to developing or refuting specific points. It is a good idea at this point to record the bibliographical information about valuable sources accurately. You may need to return to the source at a later date—and nothing is more frustrating than searching for material that you know you have read when you cannot recall the source. For a book, the name of the book and the author, publisher, and date of publication are important. For a magazine, the title and author of the article, the name of the periodical, volume number, pages, and date should be recorded. It might save time later to include a brief summary or comment under the bibliographical entry for each source. This comment will refresh your memory as to how the material might be of importance to your study.

Once the important sources have been located, a more careful reading of each is in order. Careful notes should be taken at this time. The notes might include a summary of the general point of view of the article, specific issues that it raises, and facts or statements that seem pertinent. You probably have not determined what the important issues really are at this point, and you may not have determined your own point of view yet. Certainly the organization of a specific communication is not yet in your mind. Thus it is important to record the important ideas that you have read, as well as specific supporting material that seems valuable. This will allow you to look over the essence of your reading later so that you can check your judgments. If notes are not taken, important ideas and material may be forgotten and not considered.

Knowledge from listening

In the "Material for Thought and Discussion" at the end of Chapter 1, both Hugh Blair and Woodrow Wilson point out the value of communication for sharpening ideas. In talking with and listening to others we have an opportunity for evaluating ideas, bringing our own thinking into clearer focus, and finding good supporting material. These potentials in our conversations, bull sessions, and other discussions are seldom realized.

We have seen that reading can be of value to a student interested in intelligence tests, a businessman with an overtime payment problem, and a socially conscious person concerned about fluoridation. Listening to others on these topics can be just as important a source as reading. The student can ask questions in an appropriate class or talk to a psychology professor. The businessman will want to talk with individuals in his plant, and perhaps elsewhere, who are concerned with the problem. The individual interested in fluoridation may attend a lecture on the subject or chat with a dentist or health officer. These conversations are not held to let other people do the thinking, but to obtain ideas, see arguments on both sides, determine the issues, and perhaps uncover some supporting material.

The average student uses the resources of experts surrounding him to a surprisingly small degree. Successful men in business, engineering, law, and education know how important it is to go to others for information and to sharpen ideas. The student is surrounded by and has easy access to more experts in various fields than he will probably ever have again, but he seldom makes use of them in coming to conclusions on various subjects and in preparing actual communication.

Talking with others may be of special value at two stages of preparation. First, a knowledgeable person may be consulted early for guidance in how to approach the topic. The expert may point out good background sources, name the leading writers in the field, or clear muddled thinking. All of these aids will save time and effort. Second, after a proper study has been made and tentative conclusions reached, the expert may help to check the clarity of thinking, fill some gaps in issues or material, and give some confidence that sufficient knowledge has been attained for proper judgment and later communication.

Two cautions should be mentioned here. First, many people have a tendency to believe everything an expert says; these people may not make their own study but be satisfied with parroting someone else. Qualified people should be consulted for guidance and sharpening, but their ideas never should be used as a substitute for one's own study. Also, you should be cautioned about your approach to the expert. Some people ask for assistance by saying, "What do you know about intelligence tests?" or "Tell me about intelligence tests." A man who has spent a significant portion of his life studying a topic may well be greatly irritated by such an unthinking approach. However, if you make clear your interest in the topic, explain what exploring you have done, and then ask for a reasonable amount of specific help, most experts will be glad to talk with you.

We can gain ideas about a subject from listening in many situations. We can attend lectures, listen to the radio and television, talk with others over coffee, at meals, in meetings, and at various other places. Active listening is necessary, of course, to tie what is being said to our experience and our desires and goals. We should question, raise objections, and argue against statements with which we disagree, all by way of sharpening our own thinking.

DRAWING TENTATIVE CONCLUSIONS

All during his reading and listening the prospective communicator should be doing some analysis—bringing his study into some focus. He should be asking questions of himself and perhaps receiving some answers. For instance, the student interested in intelligence tests may decide that some important questions are: What are intelligence tests? What are their purposes? How are they used? How reliable are they? What are their weaknesses? In what situations might they be of value? The businessman analyzing overtime costs might make judgments based on the questions: What are the causes for the increase? Are these causes controllable? What influence does the increase have on the profit picture? What areas show the greatest potential for reduction? Are the possible remedies more costly than the present situation? The fluoridation topic might lead a speaker to these early questions: What is it? Where has it been employed? Has it been effective? How effective? How valid are the arguments against it? What methods have been employed to get fluoridation into communities where it now exists?

If you do not constantly ask yourself questions like these, you are likely to make a common mistake: to determine your point of view too early and without proper foundation so that you only see ideas and materials that support your notion. This could easily mean a coloring of all reading and listening and result in your overlooking good arguments and effective supporting material. The analysis, the asking of questions, is a method of arriving at tentative conclusions and testing to see whether the material at hand supports those conclusions.

The conclusions that we draw at this time may not be used directly in a communication situation. At this level we are merely arriving at answers for our own benefit; we are analyzing and testing our knowledge.

CONCLUSION

The more informed a person is on a topic, the more difficult communication may become because he understands the complications and cannot draw simple conclusions. However, the more informed he is, the better the ultimate communication will be. Ideas stem from knowledge, and ideas are the basis for effective communication.

There are three main sources of information on any given subject. The first source is ourselves, our experience, our past reading, and our contacts with others. We should constantly strive to attach meaning to all of these activities. This source is usually a limited one, and alone it is seldom sufficient for effective communication.

The second source is reading, and generally we must do considerable reading before we are ready to communicate.

The third source is listening to others to obtain ideas or information, and to sharpen our own thinking.

It is important to analyze and evaluate the material gathered from these sources. We should never start out with our conclusion already drawn, looking only for material that supports it. Our study should open up the subject so that we can reach some tentative conclusions supported by adequate information.

REVIEW QUESTIONS

1. What sources of information are available to the communicator?
2. What aids does the library offer in locating particular information that may be needed for communication?

3. What is necessary beyond gathering information before one is ready to communicate?

PROJECTS

1. Make a bibliography of three books and of six magazine articles from at least two indices on the subject of:
   (a) the effects of automation
   (b) the role of liberal arts in education

2. From the periodical department of your library, list five periodicals with which you are familiar, five whose names are more or less familiar to you, and ten of which you have never heard. (The value of this exercise is not, of course, in the making of the lists. In making the lists you will become aware of the tremendous variety of information that is available to you in a library.)

3. Which of the following—periodicals, books, newspapers, or other individuals—*might* be the main source of material on the following topics:
   (a) why student government does not play a larger role on this campus
   (b) the role of the government in business
   (c) the present use of television in college classrooms
   (d) the possible unfairness in a recent criminal court case
   (e) the role of the state university in this state's educational future

4. Make a list of three topics on which you might expect to make some future communication. For each topic list at least three people in your college or your home community who might know more about the topic than you, and from whom you could obtain some information.

MATERIAL FOR THOUGHT AND DISCUSSION

My aim, then, is the education of the perfect orator. The first essential for such an one is that he should be a good man, and consequently we demand of him not merely the possession of exceptional gifts of speech, but of all the excellences of character as well. For I will not admit that the principles of upright and honourable living should, as some have held, be regarded as the peculiar concern of philosophy. The man who can really play his part as a citizen and is capable of meeting the demands both of public and private business, the man who can guide a state by his counsels, give it a firm basis by his legislation and purge its vices by his decisions as a judge, is assuredly no other than the orator of our quest. Wherefore, although I admit I shall make use of certain of the principles laid down in philosophical textbooks, I would insist that such principles have a just claim to form part of the subject matter of this work and do actually belong to the art of oratory. (*Quintilian,* The Institutio Oratoria of Quintilian, *tr. by H. E. Butler. Cambridge: Harvard University Press, 1953, Vol. I, pp. 9–11.*)

So, the speaker must master his subject. That means that all facts must be collected, arranged, studied, digested—not only data on one side, but material on the other side and on every side—all of it. And be sure they are facts, not mere assumptions or unproved assertions. Take nothing for granted.

Therefore check up and reverify every item. This means pains-taking research, but what of it?—are you not proposing to inform, instruct, and advise your fellow citizens? Are you not setting yourself up as a teacher and counselor of the public?

Having assembled and marshalled the facts of any problem, think out for yourself the solution those facts compel. Thus your speech will have originality and personal force—it will be vital and compelling. There will be you in it. (*Albert J. Beveridge,* The Art of Public Speaking. *Boston: Houghton Mifflin, 1924, pp. 26–27.*)

. . . [This chapter] contained a brief, working definition of communication: "the process of sending and receiving messages." Brief and imprecise as this definition admittedly is, it suggests several implications of practical importance to the business manager:

1. In the sense used here, the word "message" does *not* mean

"idea," or "thought," or "information." It means only the *physical signals* . . . transmitted between message-sender and message-receiver. Particularly significant for the business man is the fact that mere emission of talk, or of written words, or of graphic symbols does not—in itself—guarantee that anyone understands or accepts the message-sender's ideas. . . .

Indeed, one of the most dangerous and one of the most prevalent fallacies concerning communication appears to be the supposition that ideas or thoughts are literally transmitted from one person to another. It must be emphasized again that only the physical signals are actually sent or received. The receiver of the message must translate these signals into terms which are *meaningful to him.* This meaning stirred up in the mind of the receiver may or may not be reasonably close to the meaning in the mind of the sender. The mere physical reception of a message (hearing sounds, or seeing objects) is not at all the same thing as understanding it. Understanding depends upon the *receiver's* translation. A useful axiom, then, for the . . . communicator is: only physical signals are literally transmitted, never meanings.

2. A corollary of this line of reasoning is that the only message that counts in terms of what the receiver does is the message *received*—not the message sent. How fruitless the common complaint: "But I *told* him that over and over again." The crucial question is: "What did he understand (i.e., how did he interpret the message received)?"

3. A third implication is that messages may be unintentional as well as intentional. Tone of voice, manner of dress, facial expression, office furniture—these are just a few of the ways in which a person may be transmitting messages that he would prefer not to transmit.

4. By the same token, messages may obviously be nonverbal as well as verbal; that is, there are many ways of sending messages besides the use of language. The old proverb about actions speaking louder than words doubtless expresses a universal truth. . . .

5. Silence (when utterance is expected) and inaction (when action is expected) constitute messages just as truly as do words or overt behavior. In fact, *anything interpreted* by a person is, to that person, a message. Communication is always going on, then, whether one desires it or not—so long as there is someone to inter-

pret what we say, or fail to say, or do, or fail to do. Business managers, especially, need to grasp the fact that they are always communicating something to someone in the organization.

6. Any person who happens to be in the right place at the right time may receive a message intended for someone else. Therefore, message-senders should bear in mind that there are frequently unintended receivers as well as unintended messages. In a business organization the accidental information leaked from a secretary to those for whom the message was not intended can indeed play havoc.

7. The message as finally interpreted by the receiver can never be identical with the message as conceived and transmitted by the sender. Of course, much of the time the two messages are similar enough that the world's work gets done. But any message-sender should be constantly aware that what he says (or wants to say—which may not be the same as what he says) can never mean exactly the same thing to his audience as it does to him, since the receivers cannot possibly have lived his life and therefore must use different experiences in translating his words. As William H. Whyte, Jr., and the editors of *Fortune* said so succinctly in their series of articles on business communication, "The great enemy of communication . . . is the illusion of it."

8. As soon as the receiver of a specified message has received and assimilated that message, he immediately is impelled to respond in some manner. This response, if it is in any way overt, then becomes another message—usually (although not always) directed to the sender of the original message; such a response is commonly called *feedback,* assuming that the original message-sender receives it. Frequently feedback messages consist of nothing more than a slight nod of the head or a frown, but the original message-sender ignores them at his peril. . . . (*W. Charles Redding and George A. Sanborn,* Business and Industrial Communication: A Source Book, *pp. 30–32.*)[1]

A person will accept a communication as authoritative only when four conditions simultaneously obtain: (a) he can and does under-

[1] Copyright © 1964 by W. Charles Redding and George A. Sanborn. Reprinted by permission of Harper & Row, Publishers.

stand the communication; (b) *at the time of his decision* he believes that it is not inconsistent with the purpose of the organization; (c) *at the time of his decision,* he believes it to be compatible with his personal interest as a whole; and (d) he is able mentally and physically to comply with it. (*Chester I. Barnard,* The Functions of the Executive, *Cambridge: Harvard University Press, 1938, p. 165.*)

5

Aristotle believed, and practically all writers since that time have concurred, that the audience determines the speech's end and object.—Thonssen and Baird[1]

UNDERSTANDING THE LISTENER

Fortune magazine, in an article entitled, "Is Anybody Listening?," identifies one of the main problems in communication with these words:

> On this point serious students of communication are in agreement; the great gap is the gap in background, experience, and motivations between ourselves and those with whom we would communicate.[2]

Previous chapters have stressed the fact that consideration of what the listener brings to the communication situation is of prime importance in effective speaking. Unfortunately, this fact is often overlooked, forgotten, or minimized. The speaker is often too involved in what he wishes to say from his own point of view, and with his own interests and background as a basis. He therefore forgets that merely saying what he wants to say does not necessarily achieve the main goal of communication—the evoking of a specific response in a listener. An understanding of the listener is a prerequisite to the efficient and effective achievement of that response.

[1] From Lester Thonssen and A. Craig Baird, *Speech Criticism* (New York: Ronald Press, 1948), p. 15.

[2] "Is Anybody Listening?," *Fortune* (September 1950), p. 83.

The speaker must never give up the privilege and the responsibility of determining the ultimate goal he seeks. However, in determining what can and should be said at a given time, and just how it may best be said, he must study the listener carefully. The listener's background, interests, desires, and motivations will determine how the topic should be approached, what material should be used, how it should be organized, and even—on occasion—the style of presentation.

Understanding the listener is not always a formidable task. We communicate mostly with people we know well. If we acquire the habit of stopping momentarily to consider what we know about the listener, we can usually make good judgments of his attitudes, his knowledge, his communication skills, and the role he may be playing. This momentary reflection can determine our approach for successful communication with him; with some close associates we make the analysis automatically.

When our listeners are not so well known to us, we must gather as much information as possible about the listeners so that we can make predictions about their reactions. Predictability in these instances is not an exact science, and we will make errors, but the chances of error will be greatly reduced if we find out what we can about our listeners.

Occasionally we may find ourselves unexpectedly communicating with comparative strangers. In such circumstances, we must take advantage of any opportunity offered by the situation to analyze our hearers. The sexes and ages represented will probably be more or less obvious. It may be possible to pick up some clues from the contributions that others make to the discussion, or from the reactions of members of the group to what is being said. Sometimes it is possible to ask direct questions in the communication itself.

Whatever the circumstances, the person who really wants to move his hearer or hearers to make a particular response as a result of his communication must explore every opportunity for learning about those whom he wishes to influence.

FACTORS IN PREDICTING LISTENER REACTION

Let us examine some of the major factors to be considered in predicting a listener's attitudes, background, interests, and roles. The factors include age, sex, occupation, education, membership in organizations, and socio-economic level.

Age

If you were to talk to a pre-teenage group, a teenage group, and a local service club on the many pressures on college people, you might well expect three different sets of attitudes, knowledge, and motivations. Each group would require a different communication; even if the same response were sought from each audience, the approaches would vary widely. Perhaps even different responses should be sought from the three groups.

The same holds true for most topics. If the topic is education, teenagers might be more interested in immediate matters, such as getting rid of one teacher, or changing some rules around the school, or ideas on how to be accepted into college. An older group might be interested in the tax problem in supporting education, the over-all quality of education in a school, or the future of education. The teenage group will have little experience and generally no real interest in the problems facing the state legislature. Service club members may be quite interested in bills that affect their businesses but have little or no interest in some other measures. Many sociologists and psychologists have pointed out that one of the prime causes of parent-child problems is inability to communicate because of the difference in age, which implies differences in experience, desires, and motivations. Every younger person has probably said at one time or another, "My father and mother do not understand me and my world!" This may be true, but the recognition of the difference and an awareness of problems in communication might help each to understand the other better.

Sex differences

Although men, women, boys, and girls, have many interests and attitudes in common, where there *is* a difference, it *makes* a difference. Consider, for instance, the experience, attitudes, and vocabulary of each sex concerning such obvious topics as cars, clothes, and sports. The difference permeates many other areas also. Many young men are quite conscious of the fact that their college education is preparing them for a life's work, while young women know that, in general, they may work for only a short period of time before raising a family. Young men know that military service may interrupt their planned progress toward a certain goal, whereas young women do not face this particular problem.

Occupation or future occupation

Members of management and labor often find real differences in their attitudes toward the economics of industry. Teachers and lawyers may have different attitudes toward the problems of youth. Social scientists and physical scientists may not always see eye to eye on problems of government and social welfare. Engineers and salesmen often bring totally different backgrounds to the study of a manufacturing process.

These same differences can be found on a college campus where people are preparing for different kinds of occupations. The future engineer and the future marketing man, the artist and the economics major, the English major and the future chemist, may by interest and background bring considerable differences in attitudes, roles, and motivations to various topics.

Education

Both formal education and education by experience are important to consider when analyzing a listener. Knowledge of a listener's formal education will help to determine how much background material needs to be presented on such topics as government procedures, economics of the world, English literature, and various philosophies of life. Individuals with considerable formal education can probably grasp concepts more readily than those with little education. However, both general knowledge and the ability to conceptualize can be gained by experience, and formal education alone may not be the key. The important idea is that if the speaker has knowledge of both the formal and experiential education of the listener he can better make predictions about the level of understanding on which the listener should be approached.

Membership in organizations

Knowing what organizations the listener belongs to might assist the communicator in determining the listener's interests and motivations. Membership in current protest groups, service clubs, factional political groups, professional groups, veteran's organizations, library groups, or hospital organizations may indicate some of the listener's interests and motivations. Membership in no organizations could also be a clue.

On the college campus, a student whose activities are primarily in the political area may bring to a communication situation different background and drives from those brought by someone whose sole extra-curricular activities are with the outing club or the theater group. The engineer whose major activities, if any, are solely within the engineering area probably has different motivations and attitudes from those of the engineer who is active on the newspaper or in campus politics.

Socio-economic level

Often goals and motivations change as an individual achieves success in the areas of money and status. The tendency to keep what one has and to continue to progress in certain lines seems to be much greater as one rises on the socio-economic scale.

The student whose argument for off-campus living is that it saves money will have greater success before students with small incomes than before students with generous allowances from home. The statement that "all people are born liberals but become more conservative as they accumulate worldly goods" is too general to be true, but it has some basis in fact.

These factors are only hints or guides toward understanding the listener. There is nothing infallible about them. Not all 22-year-old engineers who are college seniors, come from well-to-do homes, belong to the same fraternity, and have been elected to a student government office, have the same interests and motivations. However, carefully gathered information carefully used will give the speaker more to work with than no information at all.

Information concerning specific attitudes, motivations, and background of any listener or listeners is always available if one will spend the time and energy necessary to collect it. This expenditure can pay large dividends and make the difference between effective and ineffective communication.

RELATIONSHIPS OF SPEAKER, LISTENER, AND TOPIC

The information collected about prospective listeners must be organized to be useful in predicting how the listeners will react. One pattern of organization is offered here.

The speaker should make some judgments about his listeners in five major areas: (1) What will the listener's attitude be toward the proposed response? (2) What will the listener's attitude be toward the speaker? (3) What knowledge of the subject does the listener have? (4) What experiences does the listener have that are applicable to the present situation? (5) What is the mood of the listener?

Listener's attitude toward proposed response

It is quite natural for an individual who is greatly interested in a subject to assume without thinking that others are as interested as he. The speaker may fail to realize that others may hold a different point of view on the subject. He may even understand that a listener holds a different opinion, but not feel that it is important to adapt to that difference. Such lack of consideration for the listener's interest and attitude can seriously handicap communication.

If we could show an attitude graphically, a listener's feeling toward a proposed response might fall somewhere on this continuum:

Opposed	*Neutral or Uninterested*	*For*

If the listener's attitude is to the right of the middle of this line, the speaker might concentrate primarily on strengthening this belief so that it might lead to some immediate or delayed action. Or, if the speaker decides that the favorable attitude is not very solidly based, he could give the listener solid reasons and support to strengthen his current point of view.

The speaker may determine, however, that the listener's attitude falls somewhere in the middle of the line. He must then determine the reason for this lack of interest. Is it because the topic seems irrelevant to the hearer's life? Is it because he does not have sufficient knowledge to arrive at a conclusion? Or, is it that he sees both sides of the question and has not yet made up his mind? Each of these attitudes would require a different communication to get a particular response. If the listener is uninterested, considerable time and effort must be spent to show why the topic affects him. If he is interested, but does not have sufficient knowledge, adequate background for basing a decision must be presented. If the listener is knowledgeable but has not yet made up his mind, the speaker may do one of two things: (1) answer his objections to the idea; or (2) strengthen the points already in the listener's mind to help bring about the response sought. The important idea here is that differences in reasons behind an attitude call for quite different approaches to the listener.

The attitude of some listeners may fall toward the left of the continuum. This makes communication even more difficult, but several paths are open to the speaker.

Several separate communications may have to be made before a man can be persuaded to change his opinion. For instance, if a student is interested in influencing a fellow student to accept a new form of student government, the first communication may merely present the problems of the present situation. If the speaker tried to do more than this, the listener might become defensive and not see the problems clearly. A second communication, later, might present several possible solutions to the problems, and a third communication could point out the weaknesses in some solutions and the strengths of the new form desired by the speaker. If time is available and the listener will follow actively, all of these purposes might be accomplished in one speech. However, the time available between these communications will give the listener an opportunity to think the situation through. He might otherwise feel that too prompt a change in opinion would make it appear that he was being "railroaded." The slower process can often succeed in overcoming opposition where a one-time communication might fail.

Another method of handling a listener who is opposed to an idea is first to seek areas of agreement, with a discussion of the areas of disagreement following. If the disagreements are discussed first, the listener may close his mind to any change. If you want a friend of the opposite political party to vote for your candidate, you could first seek agreement on the qualifications that a candidate for the office should have. It might then be possible to show that your candidate fits the qualifications better than his opponent. Obviously, if the listener is too emotionally involved with one party, even this method will fail.

A third way of handling a listener who is opposed to your idea is to determine what his objections are. This may be done by analysis beforehand, or you may ask the listener to state his objections. When the objections are clear, they may be answered—or at least the important ones. If the listener's mind is open to an adequate argument, he may be led to change his opinion.

Again, the important suggestion is to determine the listener's attitude so that the most successful of several approaches may become apparent. If the speaker is unaware of the listener's attitude, he may blunder into an approach that has little chance of success, and may even increase the listener's opposition.

A natural question at this point is, What if there is a group of listeners and their attitudes toward a specific response vary greatly? This is one of the problems that make public speaking more difficult than communication when only one or two listeners are involved. The answer depends on what the speaker hopes to accomplish. The speaker may want to win as many people as possible to his side; if so, he will probably concentrate on the individuals who are neutral and those who are slightly opposed. If he desires as much action as possible, he will concentrate on those already in favor of the idea and perhaps on the undecided individuals. If certain people in the group are highly respected by the others and he can win them to his side, the others may follow later. The speaker's plan then would be to determine the attitude of the respected leaders and concentrate on getting them to accept his proposed response.

Many approaches are open to the speaker. His analysis of the listeners will help in determining which is most likely to make his communication effective.

Attitude toward the speaker

Aristotle said that the esteem in which the listeners hold the speaker might be called the most potent of all the means to persuasion. If your listeners *want* to believe you, they will accept almost anything you say. Confidence in the speaker can come from two sources: the listeners' previous knowledge of the speaker, and the speech itself.

Many of your communications are with people who know

you well—in the dormitory, at committee meetings, in organizations to which you belong. Men in business and the professions also communicate primarily with individuals whom they know and who know them. If you are respected by your listeners, your communication will have their respect too. If, however, you must communicate with people who do not respect you, the communication itself will have to gain the respect needed for the occasion.

You will also find yourself in situations where you are not personally known, but where your reputation has preceded you because you are well known on campus, in the company, or the community. Again, if this reputation is favorable, you have an advantage; if it is not favorable, the communication itself must do the job.

In still other situations, neither you nor your reputation is known before you start to communicate, but someone in the group introduces you. That introduction may be no more than, "I brought Joe Smith along with me tonight," or "Joe Smith is interested in what we are talking about." You may be neither helped nor hindered by such remarks. However, if someone says, "Joe Smith has had a lot of experience in student government," you may get a more attentive hearing from the listeners. If the introduction explains your experience, knowledge, or background more specifically, it can lend considerable weight to your words. Part of the success of such remarks depends on who says them. If your friend is a respected member of the group, he will carry more weight than if he is not well liked.

In public speaking situations, you may receive a formal introduction before you make a speech. Here again, the better the introduction you receive, the more respect you start with.

If you do not think that your listeners are aware of your qualifications, or that they respect you, you may do several things in the communication itself to assist in developing in the listeners a favorable personal attitude toward you. You may include in your introductory remarks or early in the body of the speech some casual references to your background and experience. Such material must be handled carefully so that you do not appear to be egotistical, or you may bring about an effect opposite from that intended.

Another method of gaining the proper listener attitude toward you is to include a telling point early in the communication. The point chosen might well come later in the presentation under ordinary circumstances, but if a change of audience attitude is needed, it should be used early. An interesting or original idea or some support that shows the depth of your knowledge may change a passive or antagonistic attitude to a favorable one.

The speaker's physical delivery can also assist in presenting him in the right light. A hesitant, unorganized, unanimated delivery could be interpreted by a listener as signifying a lack of ideas, material, or interest. We shall discuss delivery in more detail in Chapter 10.

Knowledge of the subject

The speaker who merely repeats what the listeners already know, or who speaks over their heads, will soon find no one paying attention to him. Effective communication therefore requires the speaker to ascertain the general level of knowledge of his listeners on the specific topic under discussion.

Factors that we have discussed earlier in this chapter, like age, sex, and education, may give the speaker some clues concerning what his hearers might be expected to know. Previous experience with similar listeners may aid him in predicting the amount of information commanded by his audience. In addition, the speaker can make some direct inquiries into the matter, either by asking someone who knows them well or by asking the listeners themselves. These informal inquiries may take place either before the communication or as a part of it. Many individuals who mistakenly think of communication as a one-way affair—the speaker speaking and the listener listening, feel that any break in this pattern is bad. This is not necessarily true. Thus, the speaker may have his listeners ask or answer questions during a communication, and these questions and answers will help him determine their level of knowledge. Also, the speaker should be aware of signals that the listeners are sending to him. A quickening of interest at the mention of a name or theory usually means that the audience is familiar with it. Obvious inattention, on the other hand, probably means that the speaker's material is either so familiar as to be tiresome to the group or too abstract or technical for them.

Experience that is applicable

In addition to finding out what the listener knows, the speaker would do well to know how the experience of the hearers relates to his topic. Our meanings grow out of our experience, so if the speaker can tie his ideas to something that the listeners have already experienced, understanding and acceptance will come faster. This is particularly true when the topic involves something outside the normal experience of the listener. For instance, the speaker who explains the cost of electricity in terms of kilowatt hours will receive little understanding from an average listener. If, however, he says that using a radio costs about one cigarette a day, cooking an average meal costs three cigarettes, and using a reading lamp for two hours costs four cigarettes, the meaning comes closer to the listener's experience.

Mood of the listener

Many factors can affect the listener's attentiveness—the time of day, a difficult examination just written or coming up, the amount of sleep he had the night before, how long he has been listening to the communication, an emotional disturbance just prior to the meeting. There are times when we cannot communicate with certain individuals because of a mood brought on by outside factors. The speaker who blunders into a communication situation unaware of such a mood may be greatly surprised by his inability to get an idea across.

The communicator should use the verbal and nonverbal feedback present in all communication situations to apprise himself of the mood of the listener. The preliminary remarks before a meeting starts, the communication that precedes yours, facial expressions, posture, and signs of inattentiveness—such indications of mood help the speaker to decide what approach he should use to achieve his goals.

Occasionally the mood of the listeners is so unpropitious that communication should be postponed. For instance, at a house committee meeting you may wish to bring up a controversial topic. If emotions are highly aroused by another discussion in the meeting, you may feel that communication at this time is hazardous.

The speaker can change the mood of the listener by opening his communication with an illustration or some startling fact that will alter the listener's outlook. He might then point out the effect of his idea on the listener, or in some other way bring the listener to a point where communication is possible.

You may be saying to yourself, "Answering all of these questions about my listeners makes good sense, and is all very fine in theory, but who has time to do it?" In most cases the speaker will discover that he knows the answers to many of these questions if he only stops to think. It does not take long. Even those occasions when obtaining answers requires time and effort, the investment will pay good dividends. Compare the time spent in analyzing the listener with the time lost when no communication takes place, when points and support must be changed and repeated, or when ineffective communication leads to responses contrary to those desired by the speaker. Ineffective communication can be costly, and there are no shortcuts to successful communication.

WHAT MOTIVATES PEOPLE TO RESPOND?

One of the most controversial subjects of contemporary life is motivational research. There are those who feel that we do not know, and never will know, enough about people's motivations to discuss the matter. Others feel that motivational research is immoral because it might lead to control of individuals without their knowledge or consent.

However, any individual who spends a little time studying himself knows that he has certain needs and desires. He knows that when they are strong enough he will spend the time and energy, suffer inconvenience, and give up other less desirable (to him) needs in order to achieve his goals. The discussion of consequences as a portion of the communication process in Chapter 2 developed this idea more fully.

Various individuals have attempted to categorize these needs, desires, drives, or motives. The actual listing itself is not as important as is understanding the fact that motives exist and communication can easily fail if they are not considered. A set of drives or motives will be discussed here to illustrate how motive appeals may be planned.

The need to be known and appreciated

There have been many protests lately against the number system that automatic devices are forcing upon us. A person is a number to the telephone company, to Social Security, to the Internal Revenue Service, to his university or employer, and to other groups and organizations. The protests usually recognize the efficiency that results from such a procedure, but speak loudly against the loss of individuality. Many university students resent being mere seat numbers in a large class for roll call and examination purposes. The battle against conformity that many people wage is basically against the loss of individuality.

Each individual finds himself in many groups. In some of these he will accept being just a member with no particular personal distinction. In other groups, however, he may wish to show up as more of an individual. He may speak in meetings, ask for committee assignments, build displays, help with fund drives, or assist with the Little League club sponsored by the organization. He may be really interested in these assignments; but part of his motivation is the need for recognition by others that he is present, that he is a person and not simply a name on a roll or a body at a meeting.

The speaker needs to be aware of this potential. There may be logical reasons why students should study harder, why individuals should work hard on a certain project, should keep physically fit, and should strive for advancement. But these reasons may not motivate certain listeners at certain times. These same people might well respond to these reasons, though, if they see the possibility of gaining recognition as individuals in addition to the logical goals. At times listeners will respond negatively to good suggestions if they feel that compliance will only make them more unidentifiable as members of the group.

Like all of the motives that we will discuss here, the strength of this appeal will vary from individual to individual and within the individual from one time to another. The motives are present, however, and good listener analysis can teach the speaker how to take advantage of them in any given situation.

The need to achieve and be recognized

This need goes beyond mere recognition as a human being with some individuality. Achievement and recognition give the individual status in the group. "You are the best in the group;" "You did a good job;" "We couldn't have got along without you;" or a mere "Thank you" are often magic words.

This motive explains many of our activities. High grades are often an incentive for a student not because they mean he has mastered the content of a course, but because they are the outward sign of a type of achievement. Contests are a favorite method of increasing interest and activity in industry; the prize is often of no great monetary value, but the recognition of achievement serves as the motive. Individuals seek to be members of certain societies not because of the greater opportunity to serve but because of the recognition involved. We may award titles such as Assistant Chairman in some instances not because they have great meaning but because they reward the individual for certain achievements. A communicator should be aware of the potential of this motive.

The need for growth

Many individuals feel stifled and restricted by routine work. They are constantly looking for new opportunities to improve their talents and use their potential. Students may not be motivated to attend class if they feel that they can learn what they want to know about the subject from a textbook. The newest approach in industry is to give the members of management as much opportunity for individual determination of goals as possible so that they may grow and develop. The swelling tide of individuals taking credit and noncredit courses in adult education demonstrates the inner need of many of us to see beyond our present horizons.

A communicator may well be able to appeal to this motive in his presentation. For instance, you may be trying to get a friend or a group to join in tutoring underprivileged children, a worthy cause. In addition to pointing out the social value of the project, you might appeal to some individuals by pointing out the fact that it would give them a chance to see social conditions that they have heard about but never seen, and to gain experience in teaching. Participation in a campus club or community organization may achieve socially worthy ends, but it also gives individuals a chance to broaden their horizons by meeting different people, learning new ideas or procedures, and working in directions not a part of their normal activity.

The need to belong

One of the first research studies conducted in the motivational research area did not start out to measure motivations. In the so-called "Hawthorne studies," the amount of light and other factors were varied to determine their effect on worker produc-

of downward communication. The growth and complexity of modern industry have placed pressure upon management at all levels to develop effective means of transmitting to lower echelons information that is vital to the continuing, efficient operation of the business. The passing on of orders, policies, and plans necessary to modern industrial life is the backbone of efficient management.

Executives recognize, too, that misinformation and the resulting misunderstanding lessen working efficiency. Sharing information with subordinates at all levels of the organization tends to diminish the fears and suspicions that we all sometimes have in our work and toward our employer. This sharing affords the security and feeling of belonging so necessary for efficiency; it recognizes and fosters the pride people want to have in their work, and improves the morale and stature of the individual. Finally, effective communication helps subordinates to understand, accept, and cooperate with the frequent changes in materials, methods, and personnel that are part of modern dynamic business situations. In general, it may be said that *downward* communication is an integral part of the traditional industrial organization and is readily accepted and made use of—more or less effectively—by management. . . .

There are many values, however, that accrue to those managers who listen willingly, who urge their subordinates to talk freely and honestly. Upward communication reveals to them the degree to which ideas passed down are accepted. In addition, it stimulates employees to participate in the operation of their department or unit and, therefore, encourages them to defend the decisions and support the policies cooperatively developed with management. The opportunity for upward communication also encourages employees to contribute valuable ideas for improving departmental or company efficiency. Finally, it is through upward communication that executives and administrators learn to avert the many explosive situations which arise daily in industry. (*Earl Planty and William MacHaver, "Upward Communications: A Project in Executive Development,"* Personnel, *January 1952, pp. 304–305.*)

⁂

According to the point of view adopted in this paper communication can best be understood as a social process. All communication requires a community of at least two groups. How an individual or a group perceives and interprets the behaviour of another and the nature of the individual or group response in this interaction process can only be understood if the total social context of this behaviour is taken into account. Pigors makes this point in terms of an individual, but his observation applies also to a group. He suggests that there are three variables affecting the behaviour of the individual-in-the-social-context which are important for an understanding of communication:

(a) *What* he is. That is, his function in the total scheme of things—staff officer in cost control, line supervisor, unskilled operative, and so on. This affects his *angle of view.*

(b) *Where* he is. That is, where he comes in the social hierarchy of the particular community—at the top, in the middle, at the bottom. This affects his *scope of view.*

(c) *Who* he is. This refers to his pattern of abilities, interests, motivations, personality traits, as a person and as a member of a particular interest group. This affects his *point of view.*

These considerations are of more than theoretical interest. It follows that an individual or a group is never simply the passive recipient of instructions, information, or the content of whatever it is intended to communicate. What is communicated is restructured according to the angle, scope, and point of view of the recipient as an active agent in a process. He is not a bin into which facts are poured.

Thus the same manifest content of a communication will not mean the same thing to, and hence elicit the same response from, different individuals or groups. To take a simple example, a managerial announcement that overtime is to be worked. To the cost control officer this may mean that certain adjustments will need to be made to his calculations of labour costs. He may also decide that the extra costs will need to be offset by savings in other directions, for example, by more stringent interpretation of regulations covering allowances of various kinds. This reaction may come into conflict with the response of others in the situation, for example, the personnel manager. To the works manager the decision to work overtime may mean that he must set in motion a whole series of technical operations relating to the supply of materials, the planning of production procedures, and so on. He may welcome the decision, in the expectation of overtime enabling him to meet his production target. To the individual worker overtime may appear as a means of adding to his pay envelope (a different response to that of the cost control officer), but may also be resented as an interference with his leisure and as an added physical strain, the resentment being expressed in a determination to do as little work as possible (a response which conflicts with the expectation of the works manager). Thus one simple announcement may evoke a complex pattern of reactions, give rise to misunderstanding based on different interpretations of the same "sign" and may even result in open conflict. *(P. H. Cook, "An Examination of the Notion of Communication in Industry,"* Occupational Psychology, *January 1951, pp. 10–11.)*[3]

Too often, writers think that their job is to *write* technical reports rather than to *affect the behavior* of their readers. Television producers and theatrical directors forget that their original purpose was to affect the audience—they get too busy "putting on plays" or "filling time with programs." Teachers forget about the influence they wanted to exert on students and concentrate on "covering the material." . . . Presidents of civic and professional organizations forget they are trying to influence or affect their members—they are too busy "having meetings" or "completing programs." Agricultural extension workers forget they are trying to affect farmers and homemakers—they get too busy "giving out information" or "reporting research." *(David K. Berlo,* The Process of Communication. *New York: Holt, Rinehart, and Winston, Inc., 1960, p. 13.)*

[3] Reprinted, by permission of the editor, from *Occupational Psychology,* the Quarterly Journal of the National Institute of Industrial Psychology, 14 Welbeck St., London, W.1, England.

6

Order is the sanity of the mind, the health of the body, the peace of the city, the security of the state. As the beams to the house, as the bones to the body, so is order to all things.—Southey

ORGANIZING YOUR COMMUNICATION

We have all heard communications that were frustrating because we could not make head nor tail out of what was being said. The speaker's topic—an idea, an experience, or a problem that he was trying to communicate—may have been clear enough, and perhaps we even identified the specific response that was being sought. But the rest of the communication, on which we were asked to base a decision about complying with the response sought, was simply a jumble of ideas. Such a hodge-podge is at best ineffective in getting a response; it is also liable to misinterpretation, and the listener finds it difficult to pay attention to what is being said in these terms.

Therefore, the communicator needs to have in his own mind a pattern of development by which he can present his ideas most effectively; ideally, this pattern will also be repeated in the mind of the listener as the communication develops. Most communication has four separate but interrelated aspects: (1) some introductory comments that get the listener involved and prepared for what is to come; (2) a statement of the response desired; (3) an organized approach to the main points that explain and support the stated response; and (4) statements that bring the communication to a purposeful ending. For purposes of our discussion of these ideas, we will label the four aspects the Introduction, the Specific Response, the Body, and the Conclusion.

THE SPECIFIC RESPONSE

The specific response must be chosen first, so let us discuss it first.

Previous chapters have pointed out that understanding, acceptance, and action are the general responses sought in oral communication. These responses are broad and non-specific, and obviously the particular response in each communication must be specified: Understanding of what? Acceptance of what? What kind of action? For instance, a communication seeks an understanding of the college student's rights to freedom of speech and action. Specific responses on this topic might be what some students feel are their rights concerning freedom of speech, or the rights of students to invite controversial speakers for campus organizations. It may be that in given circumstances even these responses will be too broad and will have to be narrowed before communication begins.

Gaining acceptance on such a broad topic as, "Low grades affect you now and in the future," may be difficult because of the possible scope of the subject. This might be narrowed to, "Low grades are a symptom of poor habits that, unless corrected, will limit your future"; "Low grades mean that you are not receiving what you should from your education"; or "Low grades will limit your ability to get into a profession."

For the action response, a communication on the broad topic of how to prepare yourself for getting a job after college would probably fail. Better responses might be, "How to prepare a data sheet," "What to do before and during an employment interview," or "How to obtain the most complete information on job openings in your field."

The specific response sought in a particular communication situation must take three factors into consideration: (1) the listener's attitudes, knowledge, and experience, as determined by listener analysis; (2) the amount of time available; and (3) the future opportunities that you may have for communication with the listener on this subject.

Listener analysis and the specific response

Analysis may show that on a topic unfamiliar to his audience, the communicator will have to spend considerable time building the necessary background before proceeding to anything else. This would put a definite limit on the scope of any acceptance or action he might seek. The analysis may reveal that there is considerable opposition to the idea, and this again would limit the progress that could be made in one presentation. The analysis may show considerable lack of interest in the topic, so that much time would have to be devoted to gaining attention and involving the audience in the subject before any specific goal can be mentioned. In all these and similar instances, we can see the influence of listener analysis on the possible scope of the specific response. The speaker may wish to accomplish a great deal in his presentation because his interest in and knowledge of the topic convince him that much needs to be done. However, if the communication is to be effective, he may have to be content with a more modest goal because of the knowledge or attitudes of his listener.

A considerable portion of communication fails because speakers attempt to do too much. A skimpy coverage of many ideas then leaves the listener baffled, bored, or unconvinced. The communicator must be clearly aware of the fact that he can move no faster or farther than the listeners will allow. Otherwise he may find himself in the middle of a presentation talking at a group of non-listeners and unable to extricate himself from the hole that he has dug.

The opposite is also true, although not nearly so often. Occasionally the listener may be ready for more information at a faster pace than the speaker is presenting. Good listener analysis can also help to reduce the occurrence of these instances.

Amount of time available

The communicator must always choose his specific response in terms of the time available to him. Seldom can a speaker count on having all the time he wishes. Invitations to speak in public commonly specify specific time limits. In most communication situations, however, the speaker must be aware of the elements that help determine how long his hearers will listen. A committee meeting is scheduled to last an hour, and several items are on the agenda. Weekly dormitory meetings may last for two hours or longer, although a member has observed that after the first hour or so attention is likely to lag. In both of these situations a speaker must recognize that the importance of the topic under discussion and the time during the meeting at which the item comes up will have a bearing on how long he may reasonably take in speaking for or against a proposal. In coffee or Coke sessions, the listener who notes that most speakers are interrupted if they speak for more than a few minutes at a time will not attempt a lengthy argument. In business meetings, even if there is no time limit specified, the participants want to get back to their own jobs as soon as possible; and although they will probably be willing to listen as long as they feel the communication is making a contribution, they may be intolerant of anything they consider to be time-wasting. Even in a situation in which the topic is of interest and significance to the audience, and the group has time for a full discussion, there may be other members who wish to make themselves heard.

In all of these situations, the speaker who does not recognize the fact that he must limit his communication is likely to irritate his audience, and so make his purpose more difficult to accomplish—not only in the immediate situation but on future occasions as well.

The speaker who is aware that he has a limited time in

which to make his point may adapt to the problem in a variety of ways. He can postpone his communication to a more propitious time. He can ask for a meeting at which his topic is the sole item on the agenda. He can prepare other members of the group by talking with them before the meeting. He may wish to give them something to read before or during the communication situation that helps to prepare them for his point of view. The alert and imaginative speaker can find a variety of ways to compensate for the problem of time limits.

Future opportunities for communication

Communication situations generally repeat themselves. Committee, club and organizational meetings, business meetings, bull sessions, coffee and Coke dates, and the like, where most of our communication takes place, are repeated, often regularly.

In such situations, a communicator would be well advised not to seek his total response at one time. Listening to oral communication of any depth is not easy. The listeners need time to assimilate what has been said, and may well need time afterward to mull over the idea.

For instance, in a speech class a student may find that his best approach is to make two or more speeches to achieve a desired response. Suppose that he chooses low grades as his topic, and his research shows that there are several possible approaches. His listener analysis indicates that there is little genuine interest in the topic. Some students give lip service to their concern, but they are not ready to do very much about it. On the basis of this background, the speaker decides that the first speech should point out the effect of low grades on chances for getting into graduate school or getting a good job. The second speech might point out the reasons for low grades, and the third explain what students can do about it. The last response is the one that he really wants, but without the other two presentations, the listeners probably would not have been interested. However, the first speech or the second speech alone would have made little impact. Thus, it may take several presentations to achieve the desired goal.

The same is true in other communication situations. The listeners may be ready or willing to go only so far at a given time, but by putting several communications together, the speaker may attain the total goal he desires.

Statement of the specific response

The general rule concerning when the specific response should be stated is: When the listener is ready for it. The statement may be the first words you utter, the last statement made, or anywhere in between. However, ordinarily it should come as early as possible so that the listener will know where you are going, and can therefore follow your ideas more easily.

The introduction, as we will soon see, should gain the listener's attention and develop his interest in your topic. If this attention and interest is already present, you may disclose the response you seek at the beginning of the communication. Usually, however, an introduction must be made, and the specific response would be stated immediately afterward.

There are cases when the listener's attitude is such that an early statement would antagonize him. In the speech on low grades, the speaker who tells the listeners early in the speech that he wants them to follow a whole new study pattern may find them not interested enough to listen. In this and similar cases, the response should not be stated until sometime during the body of the presentation, or perhaps even at the end. State the desired response as early as possible, but get the listener committed as much as possible before the statement is made so that he will feel that the effect is worthwhile.

THE BODY OF THE COMMUNICATION

The purpose of the body of the communication is to develop the idea being presented in an organized fashion in order to achieve the desired response. An orderly presentation will help the listener to comprehend what is being said and to remember it for later application. Reading a magazine article or a book is of little value unless the reader can remember at least the important ideas presented. Listening to a communication is also of little value unless the substance of it can be recalled. In reading, an individual can re-read immediately if he is not sure that he understands, or he can return to the printed page later. In listening, there is only one opportunity to hear and so organization becomes especially important in any oral communication.

What points should be developed?

Research will develop many main ideas that could be used to develop the body of the communication. For instance, on the causes of low grades, all of the following are possible reasons:

- Low motivation
- Poor reading skills
  - Speed
  - Comprehension
- Lack of a proper study method
- Poor vocabulary
- Poor study conditions
- Poor background in the subject matter
- Too many outside interests
- Inability to listen well in the classroom
- Failure to seek help

Few communication situations would call for the development of all of these points. Which ones should be chosen? The points that the speaker believes, on the basis of his listener analysis, will most affect his listeners. His study and analysis may lead him to believe that the main causes for this group are lack of proper study methods and too many outside interests. In another situation, he may conclude that reading skills should be the area of concentration. The important idea in choosing which point or points to develop is to determine what will affect the listener or listeners in front of you. The amount of time allowed for your communication will be a factor, too, but the choice is always made chiefly in terms of the listeners.

How many points should be developed?

Two or three main points are usually all that can be adequately covered in a single communication. If one will do, use only one. The reasons for this are two: (1) Most people determine what they will accept or how they will act on the basis of one or two reasons; and (2) it is difficult for the average individual to comprehend and digest a considerable amount of oral communication at one time.

The reasons why people accept certain suggestions vary from person to person. Usually, however, each individual believes or acts in a particular situation for a limited number of reasons. Why take a certain course? Why join a certain organization? Why believe that Red China should not be admitted to the United Nations? The reasons may be many, but each individual usually will have one or two major reasons in his mind in each case. Finding the main reason or reasons for this particular listener or audience is the important task for the communicator. The rest of the presentation should not be cluttered with reasons and material that will seem extraneous to the listener.

The second reason for limiting the number of points covered is that we cannot easily understand and remember a great many points presented orally. Although the speaker may help the listener to comprehend and remember what has been said by the use of internal summaries as he moves from idea to idea, such aids fail if the hearer is asked to follow and remember too much. The specific number of points is not as important as remembering the ability of the audience to hear and understand.

Determining the pattern

Several differences in listeners have already been pointed out, and one more must be added. Listeners differ in the way they respond to various approaches. Some look at things more formally and objectively than others. Some are more emotional. There are those who feel that a chronological approach is interesting; others find such a method boring. A speaker may use the same points and most of the same material, but approach his organization in varying ways to adapt to the listener. Among the various approaches available to the communicator are: the chronological, the psychological, the spatial, the cause and effect, and the topical. None of these is "better" than any other; their use depends upon the topic, the situation, and the listener.

The chronological pattern. The chronological approach begins at a certain time and moves forward or backward from there. A communication showing the interference of government in labor-management relations might begin with the first significant incident where the government moved in. From this point to the present time, all or many of the significant actions on the part of the government in labor-management relations could be discussed in the order of their occurrence. A communication concerning the process involved in the splitting of the atom using the chronological pattern would take the process step-by-step in order from beginning to end.

The clarity of this method can be a real advantage. However, the speaker must be careful in its use as the listener may feel that extraneous material is being presented. Most listeners like to reach what they consider the core of the matter, and they may feel that the historical facts are not as important as what is happening now. To many people history is not a fascinating subject until it is tied to something that affects them. In using the chronological method, the speaker must be sure to tie the material presented to the interests of the listener.

The psychological pattern. In using the psychological approach, the speaker determines what about the subject matter is most important to the listener and discusses that point first, even though it might logically or chronologically seem to belong later in the presentation. If the listener is more interested in a solution to a problem than in its causes, the possible solution should be discussed early and the causes used, perhaps, to explain certain elements in the solution rather than to introduce the discussion. The listener may be most interested in what the speaker feels is a minor point. If so, and the listener is watching only for it, the unimportant point should be discussed first. It may be that the most impressive illustrations are available for a point that would logically come last in the presentation. If listener interest is weak, this point might be discussed first to get the listener involved.

The purpose behind this approach is to organize the speech according to the interests of the listener regardless of the logic involved. This does not mean that the speech should be or will be illogical, for by the conclusion all of the important points and material will have been presented. It merely uses listener interest as a starting point and builds on that interest.

The spatial pattern. Another approach has a spatial or geographical basis. For example, if the communication is intended to get the listener to use the various counseling services available on a campus, the speaker might take him on an imaginary trip through the various offices involved. A speech concerning the planets might start with the one nearest the sun and progress outward. In both instances, the listener must be interested in the subject matter if the approach is to be successful. If the listener is interested only in one counseling service, and that is mentioned last, he may be paying no attention by then. If he is interested, the listener will be shown, by means of the spatial method, an orderly approach to the possible counsel he may obtain.

The cause and effect pattern. A cause and effect approach explains why a certain problem has arisen, and demonstrates how the elimination of the cause or causes will eliminate or reduce the problem. The speaker may show that the cause of present student government problems is student apathy. If this relationship is established, he will proceed to show how apathy may be overcome and student government problems reduced. If a speaker gains acceptance for his explanation of the cause or causes of poor grades, he can then ask for action to eliminate or ameliorate these causes.

This is a very useful approach when communication concerns problems that are bothering us. Such problems result from certain causes, and it is very important for the speaker to establish this relationship. Many apparent causes are not the real causes, and it is a waste of time to try to eliminate causes that have no real relationship to the problem we are discussing. We can talk about poor study conditions; but if the real cause of low grades is lack of motivation, changes in study conditions will make little difference.

The topical pattern. The approach by topic divides the subject into logical subdivisions and discusses each. This book is an example of the topical approach. Obviously all of the topics discussed here are interrelated. We cannot separate listener analysis from organization and organization from supporting material in the final analysis. But if we tried to discuss all of these items at once in terms of their relationship, it would be quite confusing to the reader.

A communication dealing with medical care might discuss doctors, hospitals, nurses, and technicians. Obviously, each is related to the others, but some consideration of each separately may be necessary in order that the hearer may understand the interrelationship.

In most communication systems, the communicator can choose among several of these patterns for organizing his idea. He must determine from his listener analysis which of those open to him will have the best chance of success.

THE INTRODUCTION

Many communicators mistakenly assume that their listeners have the same interest in a certain subject that they have. On this basis, the speaker often proceeds to state and develop his idea to an individual or a group that does not feel involved.

As a result, little listening and even less communication takes place.

Let us take an example. Several students are gathered around a table in a snack bar for mid-afternoon refreshment. One of them has just come from a committee meeting on student government. He is excited about a new idea that has been presented there and wishes to gain the support of the others for the idea. He assumes that because it will affect them, because it will overcome some problems that he assumes all have read about in the campus newspaper, and because they are his friends, they are as interested in the idea as he is. But if he plunges headlong into the topic, he may be amazed at the lack of response.

The communicator's first task is to get the listeners involved in his idea by gaining their attention and interest. There are many methods by which this may be done.

Show why the response affects the listener

It has already been stressed that we pay attention to matters that we feel affect us. If we feel involved, we are interested. If we do not feel personally affected, even though we know that the subject is important, we cannot develop a great interest. We recognize the importance of such things as voting at election time, guaranteeing equal rights for all, and donating to the bloodmobile, but we may not feel involved enough to take action. The first job of the speaker, then, is to get the listener involved by showing that his proposals affect the listener.

This can often be done by illustrations or examples, statistics, case histories, or personal experiences that bring the subject to the personal level of the listener. The introduction must show that *the listener,* not just anyone in general, may achieve the reward, that *he* is being punished, that *his* present or future is being affected.

Arouse curiosity

The popularity of mystery books, detective stories, and television shows that stir curiosity are indications of the success of this method. What happened? How did it turn out? What would I have done? These and similar questions intrigue many people. The speaker can use this trait to his advantage.

One method of arousing curiosity is the case history approach. A brief account of an incident will often hold the listener's attention until he finds out what happened in the end. The end of the story should make a point that leads directly into the rest of the presentation. The use of an illustration or a brief example or two can arouse listener curiosity that can be used as a basis for the rest of the communication.

An important caution here is to include only necessary details. Since the listeners are interested in the end of the story or the final results, get there with all speed possible in order not to lose their curiosity.

Use a quotation

A short, provocative statement from another individual or a quotation from a poem that stirs interest is often a satisfactory way of gaining the listener's attention. Poets, writers, and speechmakers spend a great deal of time finding a turn of phrase that states an idea with succinctness and color. Churchill's "blood, sweat, toil, and tears," or John F. Kennedy's "Ask not what your country can do for you, but what you can do for your country," are famous examples. However, there are thousands of statements that get to the heart of a matter with terseness and vividness and that might gain listener interest. Such a statement appears at the opening of each chapter of this book, in hope that it will stimulate some interest in what is to follow.

Use startling statements or statistics

It may be a good idea at times to startle the listener out of his lethargy. Shocking statements or startling statistics that show the listener that he is involved whether he likes it or not may gain attention. Statements dramatizing the danger of cancer, heart disease, and other illnesses have been employed as attention-getters: "Three Americans will die of heart disease before I finish this speech."

The speaker must be careful to analyze the effect of a statement or of statistics. Sometimes they do not startle but merely create the impression that the speaker is a sensationalist. On other occasions they may so startle the listener that he concentrates only on the statistics and misses the rest of the communication.

THE CONCLUSION

The conclusion of a communication generally refers back to and underscores the specific purpose stated earlier. The type and length of the conclusion will depend a great deal on the complexity and length of the body of the presentation.

A summary will remind the listener of the main ideas that support the specific purpose. This kind of conclusion is particularly useful if a considerable amount of material has been presented and a final viewing of the whole is essential. However, if the speaker has done a good job of reviewing his ideas as he moved from one point to another, a summary conclusion might be boring.

If a plea or an emotional appeal is essential in the communication, the conclusion is a good place for it. The listeners may be prepared for such an approach at the end of the speech whereas they were not ready for it earlier.

An illustration that brings all of the ideas presented into one story can be an effective conclusion. This reviews the ideas of the presentation but in a story that holds interest.

The conclusion is likely to be the most clearly remembered portion of the communication because it comes last; therefore it should be short, well stated, and interesting.

CONCLUSION

Most communications have four separate but interrelated aspects. The first of these to be prepared is the statement of specific response. This statement is quite specific, and is determined after considering the listeners, the amount of time available, and how much needs to be accomplished in this particular communication. The specific response should be stated as early in the communication as possible, depending on the listeners' attitudes and motives.

The body of the communication can be approached in several fashions, but it is essential to determine which approach is going to be used. The types of patterns are chronological, psychological, spatial, cause and effect, and topical. The pattern chosen and the points used to develop it must be based on a consideration of the listeners.

The introduction is aimed primarily at getting the listeners involved with the idea to be presented. If they do not feel what is coming is important, they may not pay very close attention.

The conclusion should be concise and interesting, and bring the communication back to the stated specific response.

REVIEW QUESTIONS

1. What are the four major elements in the organization of a communication? Which is most important?

2. Briefly explain several patterns of development for the main discussion of a communication.

3. What are three problems that must be taken into consideration in framing the specific response that you wish to secure?

4. What is the purpose of an introduction?

PROJECTS

1. Choose the individuals least interested in the activities of your dormitory. How would you begin a communication to them to get them involved in a particular dormitory activity?

2. Analyze lectures in three different classes that you have this semester for their patterns of development. Would other patterns be possible for any or all of these lectures?

3. Read the text of a speech famous in history—Patrick Henry's "Give Me Liberty or Give Me Death," Washington's Farewell Address, Webster's Second Reply to Hayne, Lincoln's Cooper Union Address, Bryan's "Cross of Gold" speech, for example. Analyze the organization of the speech.

4. Outline three different communications using three different patterns of development that you might make to a group of prospective students and their parents.

MATERIAL FOR THOUGHT AND DISCUSSION

In speaking, there is always some end proposed, or some effect which the speaker intends to produce in the hearer. The word *eloquence,* in its greatest latitude, denotes, "that art or talent by which the discourse is adapted to its end."

All the ends of speaking are reducible to four; every speech being intended to enlighten the understanding, to please the imagination, to move the passions, or to influence the will.

Any one discourse admits only one of these ends as the principal. Nevertheless, in discoursing on a subject, many things may be introduced which are more immediately and apparently directed to some of the other ends of speaking, and not to that which is the chief intent of the whole. But then these other and immediate ends are in effect but means, and must be rendered conducive to that which is the primary intention. Accordingly, the propriety or the impropriety of the introduction of such secondary ends, will always be inferred from their subserviency or want of subserviency to that end, which is, in respect of them, the ultimate. (*George Campbell,* The Philosophy of Rhetoric. *London: W. Strahan and T. Cadell, 1776, Vol. 1, pp. 25–26.*)

In all communication, the human factor is all important. Man has a psychic need for communication—to communicate and to be communicated with, to express and to comprehend the expression of others. In order to communicate better and faster, man has applied some of his finest scientific thinking to developing the telegraph, the printing press, television and the telephone.

Without detracting from the overwhelming importance of such technological miracles, it still needs to be emphasized that true communication is less a matter of means than one of mental processes. And since there can be no communication without comprehension, it requires an active posture of thought on both sides. For all true communication is education, and all education is necessarily the consequence of communication. (*Roy E. Larsen, "Communications: Can It Help Achieve Our World Purpose?",* Printer's Ink, *November 4, 1960, p. 50.*)

In every single speech it was important to realize clearly in advance the presumable content and form of the objections to be expected in the discussion, and to pull every one of them apart in the speech itself. Here it was expedient to cite the possible objections ourselves at the outset and demonstrate their untenability; thus, the listener, even if he had come stuffed full of the objections he had been taught, but otherwise with an honest heart, was more easily won over when we disposed of the doubts that had been imprinted on his memory. The stuff that had been drummed into him was automatically refuted and his attention drawn more and more to the speech. (*Adolf Hitler,* Mein Kampf, *tr. by Ralph Manheim. Boston: Houghton Mifflin, 1943, p. 467.*)

7

A place for everything and everything in its place.
—Anon.

OUTLINING

In the previous chapter, we developed some over-all ideas concerning how to approach the organization of a specific communication. In this chapter, we will extend these ideas by considering the making of an outline that achieves a specific goal.

An outline may be (1) a mental organization that you have given consideration to for a short or a long period of time, or (2) a written plan for a communication. A written outline allows for a more careful step-by-step analysis to assure that each part is as effective as possible, but the mental outline is more often used in the give-and-take of most communication when it is impossible to write out the organization of each presentation. However, to learn facility in outline construction, the written outline should be studied and mastered first. Once careful habits are formed, they should carry over into the situations in which a written outline would be difficult if not impossible.

It is possible to prepare a tentative outline (mental or written) for more communication situations than you might think. For instance, your participation in most meetings can be considered beforehand, since frequently you know what questions are likely to be discussed. A committee meeting is called to determine reactions to a new policy ordered by the administration. A house meeting is going to consider the social events of the year. A town meeting will pass or reject a budget. A meeting of certain people in a business organization is called to introduce a new product. In these and many similar situations, you know what is going to be discussed and you can assist the effectiveness of your communication if you marshal your point of view, your reasons for that conclusion, and the supporting material to substantiate your ideas before you attend the meeting. You will have to adapt this preparation to the prevailing circumstances each time you communicate at the meeting, but some preparation, even as far as outlining, will be helpful.

Similarly, in informal and spontaneous situations, your communication will be more effective if previous preparation has made your ideas crisp, clear, and well organized. You might not know all the various subjects that might be discussed in particular situations, but you *do* know that certain beliefs and desires that you have will come up for discussion sometime. You have ideas on the role of student government, grading systems, national policies, and a myriad of other topics. If you take the time to analyze your beliefs on various matters, the reasons for or against such beliefs, and the facts that you know about them, the preparation will pay big dividends in more effective communication. Again, you will have to adapt to the particular listeners, to what has been said before, and to other prevailing circumstances. We may often say, "I didn't quite say what I meant," or "I should never had said that in the first place." If the reason for these statements is lack of previous consideration, there is little excuse. If we really believe in something, we know that we are going to communicate about it sometime, perhaps many times. Why not be mentally prepared by tentatively outlining the arguments for our beliefs before the communication takes place?

STEPS IN OUTLINING

We discussed in the previous chapter the paramount need of identifying a specific response in any communication. This clear determination of the response you seek is the first step in making an effective outline.

We also saw the necessity of determining what approach to use in the body of the speech. An outline using a space order approach to a certain topic will differ considerably from one based on the topical approach. We may change our minds during the outlining process, but we must make a tentative decision in order to begin the outline. This is the second step in outlining: determining the approach to be used.

The third step, the longest and most difficult, is choosing the main points, the sub-points, and the evidence that substantiates the sub-points so that we achieve the desired listener response. We analyze our material carefully to see all of the possible points that might help to develop the specific response chosen. From these we choose those for a particular communication with a particular group of listeners in mind.

Below is the specific response and the outline of the body of a communication made to a group of young Connecticut business and professional men. The listeners were active people, interested in matters of the day, and included in their circle of friends were many state legislators. The statements in the outline have been abbreviated for compactness. Your instructor may request a full sentence outline with source material identified. Comments are printed to the right of the outline itself.

Specific response: The members of this group should convince the members of the state legislature that capital punishment should be abolished in this state.

Outline	Comments
I. Capital punishment is not a deterrent to crime	The speaker chose this for his first point as he felt the listeners' main objection to abolishing capital punishment is that it prevents capital crimes.
A. No increase in capital crimes after abolishing capital punishment	He chose not to discuss the history of the problem, since he felt this would have little effect on this group.
1. In Minn. before and after	
2. In Del. before and after, and after reinstatement	He thought that these points (A, B,

3. In Rhode Island before and after
4. More variation in each state from year to year than before and after

C) and this evidence would be most effective of all he had available to him.

B. Comparison of similar states, one having capital punishment, the other not, shows little difference
   1. Conn. 1.3 with, R.I. 0.8 without
   2. Illinois 5.3 and Ind. 3.5 with, Wisconsin 0.9 without
   3. Vermont 1.5 with, Maine 1.6 without

As often as possible he brought Connecticut in to keep it close to home. However, he felt he must show it was generally true by going to other geographical areas.

C. People close to situation report it is not a deterrent
   1. Superior Court Judge Charles Henshel of Conn. before 1953 legislature
   2. Sir Ernest Gowers, chairman of Royal Commission on Capital Punishment who changed his mind after study
   3. Sheldon Glueck, Professor of Criminology at Harvard agrees

II. Innocent men convicted
   A. A Conn. example: Stephen White
   B. Other examples
      1. The Arthur Koes-

He chose this second point to get across a major evil of capital punishment. Because of the interest of this audience in human rights, he covered this evil first.

<table>
<tr><td>

tler book, *Reflections on Hanging,* lists page after page of examples
2. Statement of Sir Fitzroy Kelly, former Solicitor Gen. in England and chairman of the Royal Commission gives evidence to this fact

</td><td>He chose these sources from many because he felt they would be effective with the listeners. The Conn. case was chosen to be close to home.</td></tr>
<tr><td>

III. It is immoral
A. It is a vestige of the old idea of revenge
1. The Caryl Chessman Case
2. The William Edward Cook Case

</td><td>Although the speaker judged that this educated audience would be concerned with the moral aspect, he saved this theoretical and abstract point until after he had attacked the main objection and illustrated the most serious danger.</td></tr>
<tr><td>

B. Religious groups have condemned capital punishment
1. Conn. Council of Churches and the Conn. Conference of Congregational Churches favor abolition
2. The Protestant Episcopal Church of America came out against capital punishment in 1961
3. The Union of American Hebrew Congregations opposed it in 1960

</td><td>Since any general Conn. audience is likely to include members of the Catholic faith, the speaker might have adapted to his listeners better if he had included some evidence from a spokesman for this religion.</td></tr>
</table>

The introduction to this communication made reference to a recent execution that had taken place after the man had been kept in death row for years while his appeals were made, and to the bill then before the Connecticut legislature to abolish capital punishment. The conclusion reiterated the point that a bill for abolition was before the state legislature, and that many friends of those present were involved in the session and were going to vote soon on the bill.

The example given above illustrates several of the principles involved in making an outline.

Choose main points in relation to the listeners. The number of possible main arguments against capital punishment is large, but the speaker making this outline chose the ideas he used, and their order, in relation to his specific listeners. He felt that the group had heard many of the pros and cons of the problem, and he concluded that the main objection that this group might have toward abolition was that it might lead to an increase in capital crimes. He wished to allay these fears before going any further, so he chose this as his first point. If the speaker had felt that the listeners' main interest was the protection of the innocent, he would have reversed points one and two.

Other approaches might be necessary for different audiences. If the listeners were mentally asking the question, "How and why did capital punishment come about?" a time order development would have been desirable. With a different audience, it might have been necessary to point out how the listeners could best contact legislators to get them to vote for abolition. With still a different group, the immorality of revenge might be the major contention.

The main ideas to be included in an outline are determined by what will be effective with the listeners, *not* by chance or by some arbitrary choice by the speaker. What he considers important may not be effective with certain listeners.

Divide the main points into the sub-points necessary to get listener response. Many sub-points are usually available to develop main contentions. Here again, the choice is dictated by the knowledge, needs, and attitudes of the listeners.

In the outline above, one sub-point that could have been included under the first major contention (that capital punishment is not a deterrent) would be that criminals do not consider consequences when committing a crime. The speaker did not feel that this sub-point would be particularly effective with his listeners, but before a different group it might be quite effective. The same would hold true on the point in which individual opinions were cited. The speaker quoted judges to impress his audience, but before other groups he might have chosen wardens, social workers, or a combination of types of authorities.

These examples again point out the necessity for choosing both major points and sub-points in relation to the listeners instead of choosing the first thing that comes to mind, the ones you have some evidence for, or the one that seems most interesting or important to you.

Use only that material that is needed. One of the real values of outlining is to learn to check the significance of your evidence. Most successful communicators have more trouble deciding what to leave out than what to include. Good communication, as has been frequently pointed out, comes from considerable knowledge of the subject under consideration. The outline is a fine method of checking to be positive that you are including the evidence that is sufficient to achieve your goal without being boring or tiring. An outline is the best method of determining whether enough evidence is available and whether evidence included is the best possible to achieve the proper results.

The speaker who used the outline on capital punishment had much more information on the subject than he finally used in the communication. He knew how much it cost to maintain a prison inmate for a year, and how many years the average life sentence lasts; he had many other testimonials to the ineffectiveness of capital punishment, and to its immorality; he had learned a great deal about its history. He decided that this material would lengthen the presentation and not be effective in itself, and that the over-all communication would gain less response if he used it.

In choosing your supporting details, you should select the quality and quantity of information that will achieve the proper response with specific listeners.

Follow a logical sequence. An outline is not a conglomeration of points and evidence strung together by a speaker. Each major point must contribute directly to achieving the specific response chosen; each sub-point must substantiate the main point; and each bit of evidence must develop the sub-point chosen. Until you master the art of outlining you may find that, although you seem to have some logical progression because all of the material concerns the specific response chosen, in reality there is little clear organization.

The simplest and best way to check logical sequence is to add such words as, "thus," "so," "as," "since," or "because" after each main and sub-point. For example, take the following instance:

Specific response: The students of this university should petition the administration to eliminate the use of letter grades.

I. Letter grades do not give the student a clear picture of his achievement in the course
   A. Each letter grade covers too broad an area
   B. Students are refused admission to graduate schools

All the ideas stated above have something to do with the topic and might well be covered in a communication on the subject. However, they lack a logical sequence, and if we add certain words to the end of the main and sub-points, we can easily see this:

Specific response: The students of this university should petition the administration to eliminate the use of letter grades, *because*

I. Letter grades do not give the student a clear picture of his achievement, *since*
   A. Each letter grade covers too broad an area
   B. Students are refused admission to graduate school

Point "B," "Students are refused admission to graduate school," may be a strong point if adequately substantiated, but it has nothing to do with the student's receiving an unclear picture of his achievement. It should be included, if at all, in some other portion of the outline.

To return to the outline presented earlier in the chapter, the logical sequence becomes clear when we add the proper words:

I. Capital punishment is not a deterrent to crime, *since*
  A. No increase in capital crimes after abolishing capital punishment, *as*
    1. In Minnesota before and after
    2. In Delaware before and after, and after reinstatement
    3. In Rhode Island before and after
    4. More variation in each state year to year than before and after
  B. Comparison of similar states, one with capital punishment and the other not, shows little difference, *since*
    1. Conn. 1.3 with, R. I. 0.8 without
    2. Illinois 5.3 and Ind. 3.5 with, Wisconsin 0.9 without
    3. Vermont 1.5 with, Maine 1.6 without
  C. People close to the situation report it is not a deterrent, *as*
    1. Superior Court Judge Charles Henshel of Conn. before 1953 legislature
    2. Sir Ernest Gowers, chairman of Royal Commission on Capital Punishment who changed his mind after the study
    3. Dr. Sheldon Glueck, Professor of Criminology at Harvard agrees

The student of speech will do well to check the sequence of his outline, since outlines that cannot meet this test may appear to have a logical flow that they really lack.

TYPES OF OUTLINES

There are three main types of outlines: full sentence, phrase, and key word. The names themselves give a clear indication of the meaning of each type, so our discussion will be limited to the advantages and disadvantages of each.

The full sentence outline is a good style to start with in the learning process. The relationship between evidence, subpoints, and main ideas is often clearer with this type of outline. Adding the words at the end of the points to check the logic of the sequence is much easier with this style. When sources are included in this type, both student and instructor can easily check the adequacies of the sources, and the instructor can criticize the whole outline more easily. One caution should be stated, however: do not attempt to memorize this outline. Some students early in the learning process have a real fear of the speaking situation, and feel that memorization of the outline is an answer to this stage fright. It is not, and fear of forgetting what has been memorized and actual forgetting itself can seriously impair the speaker's effectiveness.

After a while, the phrase outline can accomplish most of the advantages of the full sentence outline and yet save time and keep the whole speech in view more easily. Such phrases as "Not a deterrent to crime" and "Innocent people convicted," make the essence of the point rather clear to all concerned. The danger of the phrase outline is that it is less precise and complete than the full sentence outline, and it may give the user a false sense of having clarified his idea.

The key word outline is of primary value to the speaker while he is communicating. The outline contains many fewer words, and thus it can be kept clearly in mind. If an outline is used during the presentation, the key word outline is easily seen and followed from note cards. However, if you start with this type of outline rather than the sentence variety, its lack of completeness can easily lead to lack of precision and ability to check.

CONCLUSION

Listeners can follow more easily and remember more when a speech is well organized. The need for organization leads to the necessity of learning to make an outline. An outline can be mental, but a written outline should be employed in the learning stages to make sure that proper procedures are followed. We can prepare outlines for most of the communicating we do, even in the give-and-take situation, because we usually know what subject is going to be discussed in forthcoming meetings, or we know that we have certain beliefs that we are going to express sometime.

The first step in making an outline is to identify the specific response we desire. The second step is tentatively to determine the pattern we are going to follow in the body of the communication. The third step is to choose properly the main points, sub-points, and evidence that we need to gain the indicated response from a particular group of listeners. The introduction and conclusion are prepared last.

We must choose the main points, sub-points, and material to be used with the listeners in mind. We should have more material than we can use in any given instance, and from this we choose what will be most effective with the listeners. The outline must follow a logical sequence so that the listeners can follow the presentation easily and evaluate what is being said.

There are three types of outlines: (1) full sentence, (2) phrases, and (3) key words. Usually the student should start with the full sentence outline to make sure that his points and their relationships are easily checked. The other styles may be used later. The key word outline is a good one for the speaker to use while communicating.

REVIEW QUESTIONS

1. When is a written outline more useful than a mental one? When is a mental outline more useful than a written one?

2. For what kind of communication situations can tentative outlines be prepared in advance?

3. What are the three steps in preparing an outline?

4. What is the relationship between the process of outlining and the prospective hearers of the communication?

5. What are the advantages and disadvantages of full sentence, phrase, and key word outlines?

PROJECTS

1. Analyze a couple of recent speeches made by members of this class. Were the main points chosen the ones that could have been most effective with you, or should others have been chosen? How about the sub-points? The supporting material?

2. Outline the lecture that you would have made had you been teaching the principles of organization to this class.

8

We might as well give up the fiction
That we can argue any view.
For what in me is pure Conviction
Is simple Prejudice to you.
—Phyllis McGinley[1]

SUPPORTING IDEAS AND DRAWING CONCLUSIONS

We are now prepared to discuss in some detail the rhetorical heart of communication—the evaluation of supporting ideas and their combination into sub-points, main points, and ideas. In the first three chapters and in Chapter 5, we outlined the psychological milieu in which communication takes place, and which recent research indicates is the major factor in persuasion. The manipulator, the demagogue, the man who believes that the ends justify the means can abandon further study at this point and use the insights that he has gained into the audience that he sets out to control. But the rhetorician must go further; he concerns himself not only with what does happen, but what ought to happen. And we believe that defensible techniques of social control must be grounded in reason. Therefore in Chapter 4 we gave you an introduction to this chapter, discussing sources of information and the means of

1 "Note to My Neighbor" from *Times Three* by Phyllis McGinley. Copyright 1951 by Phyllis McGinley. Originally appeared in *The New Yorker*. Reprinted by permission of the Viking Press, Inc.

drawing tentative conclusions; and in Chapters 6 and 7, on organization and outlining, we discussed the general principles of putting ideas together. We are now ready to approach directly the problems of using facts to prove an idea.

WHAT IS A FACT?

We commonly say that facts form the basis for logical argument. But when we try to define "fact" we run into difficulty. Is a fact a universal truth? Anyone who has kept up with the rapid advances in science during the past 50 years knows that today's universal truth may very well be the day after tomorrow's outmoded hypothesis; if facts are universal truths, then we have precious few of them to work with. Is a fact, then, something on which there is general agreement? If so, then it was a fact at one time that the world was flat. Also, basing a fact on general agreement raises the question of how general the agreement must be. Does it take a majority vote to establish a fact? For most of us, the posing of such questions make it uncomfortably clear that we cannot define "fact" very satisfactorily.

To provide one way out of this difficulty, let us consider a pair of technical definitions. Technical definitions are definitions that are agreed upon within a particular frame of reference. Most of us are aware of the technical definition of "labor" used in obstetrics, and of "trick" in card games; we may not be so familiar with the technical definitions of "list" in navigation and "work" in mechanics. For the purposes of our discussion, then, let us propose two technical definitions. A *fact* is something going on in the world; it is nonverbal; it is neither true nor false—it merely exists. What we ordinarily call a fact is actually a *statement about a fact;* we determine the truth or falsity of such a statement by comparing it with the fact itself.

A couple of illustrations may help to make these definitions clearer. Suppose someone asks you, "What is the color of the walls in this room?" If you are going to stick to the *fact,* in our terms, you cannot say anything in reply (a fact is nonverbal); you can only point to the wall (that which is going on in the world). Facts are not communicated; they are only experienced. As soon as you say, "The wall is green," you have moved from fact to statement about the fact. To determine whether the statement is true or false, we must compare the statement with our experience of what the wall looks like. We then may agree that the statement is true, or we may agree that it is false, or the color of the wall may possibly be so far towards blue-green or yellow-green that observers might differ as to whether it can be called green at all. You may be wondering now how we go about testing the truth or falsity of an historical statement about the fact—such as, "Columbus discovered America in 1492"—when the fact itself is impossible to retrieve. The answer is consistent with our general principle that the truth of a statement depends upon its correspondence with the fact it reports: we must go back to the reports of those who actually witnessed the fact, such as ships' logs, and diaries.

So far we have dealt with fairly simple statements. Do the things we have been saying hold true for more complicated and abstract statements, such as, "Democracy is the best form of government under which to live"? The answer is still yes. How do we decide the truth of such a statement? We must make a great many observations of what life is like under various forms of government—or gather together the observations made by others. What we know—our knowledge—is based, then, upon the kinds of statements that we make about the facts we have experienced, and our acceptance of the statements that others have made about their experiences.

You may have inferred from our definitions of "fact" and "statement about a fact" that a statement must be either true or false. Let us examine this opinion and see to what extent it of itself is true or false. There is a class of statements that approach universal truth: the sun rises in the east; all men are mortal; maple trees shed their leaves in the fall; hydrogen atoms have fewer electrons than fluorine atoms. Such statements ordinarily are composed of words whose meanings are clear, and the facts that they report reflect the regularities of nature. There is also a class of more specific statements whose truth or falsity can generally be determined with near certainty because they rely on objective standards: the Empire State Building is the tallest building in the United States; there are seven chairs in this room; no one is absent from class this morning; peas and corn have sprouted in my garden. Another class of statements will be judged true or false according to how we define terms: he is a child; you are drunk; it is a big building. We can argue at length and to no purpose about these statements until we agree on definitions of "child," "drunk," "big"; then we have established a measurement against which to determine the truth of the statement. Some statements express judgments: he is a naughty boy; that is a beautiful painting; you look best in blue. Although these statements seem to be saying something about the boy, the painting, and you, they are actually only telling us how the speaker reacts. We can judge the truth of these statements in two ways. First, we can say, "That's true" (or "not true"), by which we mean merely, "I react in the same way that you do." Or we can inquire into the reasons that lead the speaker to make the judgment; then to say that the statement is true or false means that the speaker has picked good (or bad) criteria, or that the object being judged does (or does not) exhibit the criteria.

We have thus far been talking for the most part about rather simple and uncomplicated statements because these are the ones that describe the facts—what is going on in the world. Later in the chapter we shall discuss some methods of examining statements that go beyond reports of what goes on to conclusions that we can draw on the basis of the reports.

THREE KINDS OF REPORTS

We have thus far established a difference between facts and statements about facts, and explored what we may mean when we say that a statement is true. Now let us turn our attention to the forms in which we may get statements about the facts. We shall discuss three: personal experience, the testimony of others, and one special kind of testimony—statistics.

Personal experience

Personal experience, as we shall use the term here, means statements about the fact made by the individual who actually observed the fact. The speaker who tells us what he has done and seen is reporting from his own personal experience. The report of the person who has observed the fact is as close as we can get to the fact without observing it ourselves, and therefore personal experience has great potential for being the most reliable statement about the fact that we can use, but there are some limitations to this kind of statement.

Unfortunately, we are not all accurate observers. You visited some friends within the past two weeks or so; what sort of drapes decorated the windows in that room where you spent a whole evening? How many steps do you climb from the first floor to the second floor of your dormitory? How many foreign-made cars did you see on your way to work this morning? We constantly witness things to which we do not really pay any attention.

What are the things that we really see? First, they are likely to be things that we are looking for. If you start home tomorrow with the intention of counting the number of Volkswagens you see on the way, you will notice these particular foreign cars when you see them. The chemist who is working out an experiment will notice the presence or absence of a precipitate, because it is one of the signs that indicates what his results will be. Second, we notice things that particularly interest us. An interior decorator, or a woman thinking seriously about doing over her own home, will probably notice the treatment of windows in a home that she visits. If you are an architect or an engineer, you may have counted the number of steps between floors in a building. Third, we observe through our prejudices—a special kind of "interest." A southern segregationist traveling in the North and a northern integrationist traveling in the South will each notice a variety of things that fit in with his prejudices although those same things would be so taken for granted by his counterpart that they would escape attention. Finally, we observe and remember something that calls attention to itself because of some unusual characteristic, such as size, color, activity. If those drapes had been bright orange or shocking pink, or if the steps between floors had been noticeably higher or lower than usual, we might have made a mental note of the fact. It should be clear by now that the reasons for our noting what is going on about us can distort our first-hand reports as well as give them extra force.

Testimony of others

Since we are all limited by time, space, and budget in the number of observations we can make of what is going on in the world, we must rely heavily in many of our communications on the second kind of statement about the fact: the testimony of others. We may speak confidently about hunting in Alaska, fishing in Maine, gambling in Nevada, or plumbing in Europe on the basis of what a neighbor who spent his vacation in one of those places has told us. Or we may draw on the tremendous amount of material stored up in books, magazines, and newspapers by men who have made observations that we could not make.

We must be particularly careful in using the testimony of others. Not only do we have all the problems of the authority's report of his original observation, but there is the danger that the speaker quoting the authority is reporting what was said on the basis of the *speaker's* special interests, or prejudices; the more hands through which the information passes, the more possibilities there are for interpretations to creep in. At best, you probably learned that Columbus discovered America from someone who had read a book by someone who had read a different book by someone who had actually read what Columbus had to say about the matter. There is not much danger of error creeping into this report, but what do you really know about the way in which the European settlers in this country treated the American Indians? We can test the authority of second-hand sources by asking questions about the person who made the observation. Who is he? What education, background, or experience does he have that makes him believable on this topic? How does he know? On what basis does he make his statements? What makes him think so? If he is drawing conclusions, rather than merely reporting on his own experience, do his conclusions follow from his observations? If we are to build the strongest argument possible, we must use the testimony of others, but we must also be critical of it.

Statistics

A kind of testimony that merits special attention is statistics. We use the word in a variety of senses. Sometimes we refer to any numerical report as statistics: There are 1,800 students in this college; the classroom has 35 seats; 5 people were absent; the room was 20 feet long.

There is a more technical definition of statistics. It is a method of interpreting the relative frequencies of various kinds of occurrences. We say that the "average" cost of education per pupil in one state is $325, and in another state it is $232. Or we may report that the "mode" for student credits at this school is 15 credits because more people take that number than any other number. We may "correlate" by showing that 80 per cent of the freshmen with grades below a certain figure do not graduate, thus pointing out that the chances that a freshman whose average is below this figure will finish college are very low.

Statistics themselves, if properly arrived at, do not lie, and because of this fact we are likely to have an inordinate respect for them. Figures cause problems, however, when we do not know what they mean, or when we misinterpret them. For instance, we may hear two sets of figures on the employment rate as of the same date because each individual reporting used a different definition of "unemployed." The use of the term "faculty-student ratio" in university levels has fallen into disrepute because different people use different definitions in figuring the ratio.

We must also be sure that we are comparing comparable situations when we use statistics. The drop-out rate in a state university may be 15 per cent, while a nearby small private college may have only a 4 per cent rate. We cannot therefore conclude that one school is more difficult than another, one is easier to enter, or one has poorer students than the other. Admission procedures, criteria for dropping students, costs, and many other factors make such comparisons dangerous.

We must also use caution in drawing conclusions from statistics. One state may have more state police than another and also a lower highway accident rate, but if the population densities of the two are different, we cannot conclude that more policemen make for fewer accidents. One newspaper reported that several people had drowned in a lake that had an average depth of two feet. The statistic was true, but the part of the lake in which the people had drowned was eighteen feet deep.

Because statistics are valuable in that they may bring many examples together concisely, they are often good evidence. They should be carefully examined, however, to be sure they were objectively collected, they have the same basis when comparisons are made, and the conclusions drawn are valid.

Personal experience, the testimony of others, and statistics are all forms in which statements about facts are made. If we understand the strengths and weaknesses of each, we can better evaluate their use in communication.

USE OF SUPPORTING DETAILS

Thus far we have discovered that facts—things going on in the world—are the basis of our knowledge, and that determining how accurately statements about a fact reflect what is actually going on is not a simple matter. We have also discovered three forms in which statements about facts can be presented. But this discussion has been largely theoretical and abstract. Let us see how to put these statements to work supporting an idea that we wish to communicate.

We may need to use the statements about the fact in two different ways. First, we may need to use such statements in order to make an idea clear. We may use statistics to show the extent or types of unemployment, or we may use a personal observation or the testimony of others to explain what happens in a home where unemployment has struck. Second, we may use statements about facts to strive for acceptance of our idea and resultant action, immediate or delayed. This often requires considerably more use of statements about facts, in order to be complete enough to achieve a change in attitude or belief. Whether we are using these supporting details for clarification or as evidence, we commonly use them in a form more complicated than a simple report of what is going on in the world. Let us look at three forms that supporting material may take.

Simple report

The first type of supporting material is, of course, the simple report: facts and figures. Lander, Wyoming, averages 2.7 inches of rain in March. Three students compiled a straight "A" average for the four years in college. This production line averages 80 units per hour. Bronze is a mixture of brass and tin.

Examples and illustrations

Frequently a more complicated kind of support than simple reports is necessary. Suppose you are arguing that your college should stop keeping certain records, your main point being that other colleges have done so without poor results. You might give as specific examples: a nearby school that dropped the procedure, your greatest athletic rival school, which did the same, and the outstanding school in the area, which never had the rule. In business, an individual wants his company to adopt a new procedure. He may use the following specific instances: the closest competitor recently adopted the procedure, reduced prices, and increased business; two smaller companies and one larger one nearby used the new method; a new company in the area adopted the new procedure from the beginning.

When examples are expanded, we call them illustrations. In a discussion of federal responsibility for medical care, someone may tell a detailed story of his experience under government medical care. You are discussing the lack of student participation in college activities, and you explain how you tried to get several students to join in a certain function without success. Examples and specific instances can usually be quickly reported, and thus several can be used in the same time an illustration takes. However, illustrations sometimes have an emotional appeal that is effective in communication.

Comparison and contrast

A third method of supporting an idea is by means of comparison or contrast. We might seek clarification of the size of the Pentagon by comparing it with the college campus. We might compare the onset of automation with the beginnings of the industrial revolution. We might contrast American methods of education with those in Western Europe.

Examples, illustrations, and comparison and contrast as forms of support make use of a collection of statements about the fact, and they are therefore tested by the criteria that we discussed earlier in this chapter. Since they are more complex than a simple statement, however, it seems useful to take some time to point out their use.

If it seems to you by now that the main purpose of this

chapter has been to make it appear more and more difficult to communicate accurately, you have come close to the truth. But the difficulties and complications of getting an accurate representation in words of what is going on in the world have been pointed out because most of us take statements so much for granted that we do not question them as much as we should. In spite of the fact that there are many difficulties in the way of effective communication, an awareness of the problems involved in using statements about facts can enable you to analyze such statements more carefully yourself, and to recognize errors in the ways others use them.

ARGUMENTATION

Argumentation, we have said, is based upon evidence; without having the facts, or without being sure of the accuracy or real meaning of our statements about the facts, we have no basis for building a sound argument. But we must *use* the statements about the facts—put them together in such a way that they prove our point, and this process we call "reasoning." The basic form of reasoning is induction, or generalization—drawing a general conclusion from several specific examples (observations or statements about what goes on in the world); its subsidiary and counterpart is deduction—starting with a general statement and drawing a specific conclusion from it.

We generalize when we observe several examples of a class of objects and then conclude that what is true of these examples is true of the whole class. We ride in an MG, a Volkswagen, a Renault Dauphine, and each time we are surprised at the amount of leg room in the car; we decide that small foreign cars have more leg room than one might expect. Inductively we have drawn the general conclusion, "(All) small foreign cars have a larger amount of leg room than one might expect." But suppose that some time later, having established this general principle, we reason that since such cars do have considerable leg room, a SAAB (a specific example of the class) will also have more leg room than expected. We have then reasoned deductively, from a general principle to a specific conclusion.

Induction

Induction is the basic form of reasoning. By induction, we examine several members of a class and then assume that what is true of these members is true of all members of the class. The classic induction example is testing the quality of the apples in a barrel by looking at a few of them. If we reach into the barrel and pull out several apples and all are good, we assume that the barrel contains all good apples. But there are certain pitfalls to avoid if we are to use this method validly.

First, we must examine enough examples of the class about which we are generalizing to draw a significant conclusion about the whole group. The salesman who meets three grumpy purchasing agents in a row is likely to conclude that all purchasing agents are grumpy. When a student says in a speech, "The students at this school are agreed that . . . ," his instructor may discover, by questioning him, that his generalization is based upon what the speaker and his roommate think on the subject. We can easily recognize in these cases that three purchasing agents and two students are not enough samples of their classes from which to draw a conclusion about the entire group. But it is not easy to say how many instances you need to draw a valid conclusion. The more the better, of course, and statisticians have worked out refined theories and techniques of sampling. But hasty generalization—drawing a conclusion after examining too few instances of the class—can lead to invalid results.

But suppose the student just mentioned replies, "I asked all 86 students who live on my floor, and 78 per cent of them agreed. . . ." Eighty-five is a much larger sample of the student body than two, of course, but another problem of induction is illustrated by this conclusion. Unless this student lives in a rather unusual lodging, a poll of all those who live on one floor will be limited to the opinions of either men or women students; in some schools they might be all freshmen, or almost all juniors or seniors. It is necessary in generalizing, therefore, to choose not only enough examples, but also typical examples. The sample must furnish a cross-section of the group about whom we are generalizing. If we ask all the foremen in a plant what they think about a change in production methods, and then assume that we know what the labor force thinks, we may draw an invalid conclusion, since the foremen may form an opinion on the basis of their supervisory responsibilities rather than from the point of view of the worker on the line.

There is a third check on the validity of induction. Suppose you are advocating the use of a certain advertising medium, and you point out in support of your choice the fact that four out of five of our largest competitors are using the medium, and therefore you conclude that it must be the best for companies of our sort to use. What about that fifth competitor? Is he doing well without resorting to the medium that you are proposing? If so, then we have found a negative example that casts doubt on the generalization that all successful competitors are using this medium. If students generally seem to favor an academic regulation, but a number of student leaders oppose it, then we would do well to account for the negative reaction of such outstanding students.

In checking induction, then, we must make sure that we have enough instances to provide a reliable sample, that the examples are typical of the entire group, and that there are no significant negative examples that must be accounted for.

Deduction

In deduction, we argue from a general principle to a specific application of that principle. If we complain that automation always means that people are put out of work, and therefore automation in this company will mean that some people will be fired, we are arguing deductively. The basis of the argument lies in the contention that all automation systems put people out of work. This, of course, is a generalization that must be proved inductively. One fallacy of deduction, then, is beginning with a general principle that is not true, or not true enough. There may also be a question as to whether the particular instance can be included under the general principle. Parents who argue that all children should be in bed by nine o'clock will soon be met with the counter-argument that "I am no longer a child."

Formal analysis of deduction is a complicated and technical process, and we do not believe that as brief an explanation of the syllogism as we have space for would be very useful to you. You can gain considerable insight into the problems of deduction, however, if you remember that it is arguing from a general principle, that the general principle must be true, and that the particular instance must be included in the general principle.

Minor forms of reasoning

We shall consider briefly two other kinds of reasoning: cause and effect, and analogy. Both are based on induction and/or deduction, but have special problems of their own.

Causal relations are ordinarily much more complicated than we first realize. When you were in the fifth grade, for instance, you probably learned that slavery was the cause of the Civil War. When you took the American history course in high school, you discovered that the causes were a much more complex network of economic and constitutional problems. If you have studied that era of American history in college, you have probably discovered that even the reasons given in high school were greatly simplified. In any but the simplest cases ("Step over that line and I'll punch you." "If you stop eating, you will get hungry.") almost any effect is the result of a variety of causes. We must therefore ask, in examining cause and effect reasoning, whether the alleged cause is sufficient to have caused the effect, whether it was operating, and whether there were other causes that might have had a more important part in producing the effect.

We can also predict by cause to effect. When certain

conditions have been present in the past, certain results have happened. Thus, if these factors are present now, we can predict with some degree of accuracy that certain events will occur. We use this method in predicting certain aspects of the business cycle. From past experience you have seen that if an average student gets involved in too many activities he will have scholastic problems. Thus, if your roommate begins to move in this direction, you can perhaps convince him to reduce his activities, or fail to add another, because of possible disastrous results.

Causal relationship arguments often are quite complex and involved and as a result should be used with caution and a clear understanding of the difficulties involved.

Analogy is another type of reasoning, although many rhetoricians feel it is so difficult that they minimize its value. Analogy is a comparison of the known and unknown and, by showing that essential elements in each are the same, predicting that what happens in the known situation will happen in the unknown one. If one college took a certain action with good results, and you can show that your college is the same in its essential elements, the same result is likely to happen if your school takes that action. The difficulty lies in being sure of what these essential elements are and in being sure that they are the same in both instances. As a result, the analogy is often a weak form of reasoning.

PROPOSITIONS

The general principles of organization we discussed in the last two chapters hold for all communicators. There are special considerations, however, that attach to various kinds of propositions that we may choose to advance. We shall discuss two: propositions of judgment and propositions of policy.

Propositions of judgment

The proposition of judgment asks the hearer to concur in a judgment that one has made. Some judgments are so well accepted or so self-evident that they are rarely questioned: Lincoln was a great president; motion-time studies are useful management tools; America is a great country; free public education is beneficial to the state; a voter should become informed on the issues before exercising his franchise. But there are other propositions of this same form that are hotly debatable: Brother Robbins is the best candidate for president of the fraternity; numerical grades reflect a student's progress more accurately than letter grades; a broadly based education is preferable to specialization; a picnic would be a better social event than a dance; the closed shop is an infringement of the worker's freedom; the public will receive better care under socialized medicine.

Proving a proposition of judgment always requires two steps: the setting up of criteria and the testing of the proposition against the criteria. Because the first step is commonly accomplished without our realizing it, most of us do not recognize its importance. But the criteria are always implied, if not actually expressed, in the arguments that are presented. Let us ask the question for each of the examples given at the end of the last paragraph that will lead us to specifying the criteria on which we should base a judgment. What are the qualifications that a candidate for fraternity president ought to have? What do we mean by a student's "progress"? What is the purpose of an education? What makes a successful social event? What freedoms should a worker enjoy? Of what does good medical care consist?

For instance, you might decide that a good fraternity presidential candidate is a man who has the respect of the others in the house, who has some successful executive experience, who has time to devote to the duties of the office, and who is willing to serve. If you believe that Brother Robbins possesses these qualifications and you wish others to support his candidacy, you must first convince the brothers in the house that these are the main criteria. They may feel that previous experience is not so important and that "being a good guy" is the primary requisite. You must show them that your criteria are the most important or they must convince you to accept theirs along with your own before proceeding. Until there is some agreement among those present on the qualifications needed for the office, there is little value in going to the second step.

Once criteria are agreed upon, you can discuss Brother Robbins in terms of them. You will show that he is respected, has valuable previous experience, has the time for the office, and is willing. Arguments may arise, for some of your listeners may not feel that he has the respect of the group, or may feel that his time is too restricted to run the office well. These arguments must be overcome if your specific response is to be achieved.

We are frequently not aware of the two steps necessary in proving a proposition of judgment. In the example above, suppose that someone said at the dinner table one evening, "Joe Smith would be a good president because he is such a good guy and his playing on the football team gave us some good publicity." It probably does not occur to this man that he is implying that being a good guy and giving the house good publicity are the requisites of a good president. He would probably not seriously propose such an argument if he realized what he was doing. When we understand that the reasons we give for adopting a proposition of judgment imply the criteria on which we are basing our judgment, we can review the criteria more critically and determine whether they are really significant in the context under consideration.

Thus, we can see that proving a proposition of judgment has two distinct steps: (1) establishing the criteria, and (2) applying the criteria to the situation at hand. Depending on the listeners, both of these steps may be necessary, because unless the listeners agree with both, the purpose of the communication may not be accomplished.

Propositions of policy

The second kind of proposition is one that advocates some sort of action. Sometimes explanation is all that is necessary in order to achieve understanding and acceptance, for example when a foreman explains a useful new procedure to the men under his direction, or when an academic adviser tells a student how to go about filling out his registration forms. In such cases the hearers are already highly motivated to perform the action that the speaker asks of them and instructions are all that is necessary.

But we commonly find ourselves advocating policies to which our hearers are either indifferent or opposed, and the job of communication becomes more difficult. Perhaps you want your father to let you have the car next Saturday night, or your fellow workers to sign up to donate blood when the Bloodmobile next visits your place of business, or a club to which you belong to donate $25 to the book fund of the local library, or your roommate to try writing for the school newspaper, or your boss to adopt a better accounting system, or your representative in the state legislature to support a bill for increased aid to education. In all of these situations you are seeking a specific kind of action from your hearers as a response to your communication. How should you go about getting this response?

In some of these cases a simple problem-solution development is all that is necessary. You show your club that circulation at the local library is increasing steadily, and that the book budget is far below that of other libraries in similar communities. The solution to the problem may be accepted: give money. If the majority of those present are reluctant to spend money or the constitution of the organization prohibits expending group funds for such a purpose you may not succeed, or an amendment may reduce the appropriation to $10, or—if you are very persuasive—increase it to $50. But the solution is clearly evident from the presentation of the problem.

Other topics are more complicated, and require a three-part analysis:

Need. First, you must make clear the need for doing something about the problem that you are discussing—you must create an imbalance in the minds of your hearers. Sometimes the need is clear from the start, and all you have to do is call the facts to the attention of the listeners. Most of us have heard enough these days about the wonders that whole blood and plasma can perform to be aware of the necessity for continuing supplies. In other cases you will have to work harder. You may have to go into detail to persuade your legislator that current educational opportunities in your community are not adequate; the head of your company may think that the accounting system he now uses needs no improvement. Whether you have merely to point out to your hearers a problem of which they are already aware, or must develop at some length the evidence that shows the existence of a problem, the first necessary step in a proposition of policy is to get the listeners to recognize the need for a change in the present situation.

Plan. If the need does not automatically suggest its own solution, or there are problems in the way of putting the solution into effect, or there are a variety of ways of going about it, then you must go on to a second step and present a plan for action. If your parents plan to go out on Saturday night, it is not enough to convince them that you really need the car; you must also show them that it would not be difficult for them to arrange transportation for themselves. It will do little good to point up the inadequacies of the accounting system that the company is now using unless you can suggest ways by which to improve it.

On occasion, the ease with which a plan can be put into action is clear, and thus explaining such a plan is all that is necessary to get the response you seek. Many times, however, you will need to build an argument to show that the plan is practical—that it is possible to put such a plan into action. For instance, a plan for military defense of Western Europe must show that the nations, or at least the key nations, will join the plan. A plan to increase educational grants to state communities will also increase taxes; besides, the speaker must show the probability of getting such action through a state legislature. A plan to overcome financial losses in a city bus company by raising fares must show that approximately the same number of people will use the buses. A plan to show an increase in educational benefits in a college by lowering the student-faculty ratio must show that the money and the personnel to accomplish the plan are available.

Benefits. A third step may be necessary to inspire action on some propositions of policy, particularly if the general topic or the proposed plan is complicated. You may have to point out specifically the benefits that adoption of the plan will bring about. Ordinarily this will mean that you will show how the plan will meet the needs that you pointed out earlier. This step may be necessary particularly if you have developed your ideas through a series of presentations to the same group of listeners; they may have forgotten some of the needs that you presented to get them interested in the problem in the first place. Sometimes the benefits will go beyond the limits of the topic. Assure the legislator that his support of the education bill you favor will help him to win or keep your vote in the next election. Point out to your roommate that his excursion into campus journalism would not only help the newspaper but also broaden his contacts and experience, and so provide benefits for him personally. Tell your employer that the new accounting system that you propose would not only overcome the errors in the present system, but also allow a greater breakdown of costs without increasing expenditures.

CONCLUSION

In this chapter we have surveyed in a highly condensed form the elements of logical proof: evidence and reasoning, plus two types of propositions. We have traced argument back to its source in statements about the facts—verbal reflections of what is going on in the world. We have discussed the kinds of expression that these statements may take, and the forms in which they become supporting materials. We have seen the most common forms of reasoning, and discovered sources of invalidity in them. But at best all we have been able to do in so brief a presentation is to find some hints about the kinds of things to look for in evaluating the logical bases of communication. Only when you have accumulated a good deal of experience in ferreting them out in actual practice will this chapter be fully meaningful.

There are two types of propositions in communication. One is a proposition of judgment, and the development of this type of proposition consists of two steps: (1) establishing the criteria and receiving agreement on them, and (2) applying the proposition to the criteria. The second type of proposition is a proposition of policy. The steps involved in this type of proposition are: (1) showing that there is a need for a change from the present method, (2) presenting a plan that is practical, and (3) showing that the plan at least fulfills the need, and that it may have additional benefits as well.

REVIEW QUESTIONS

1. Distinguish between a fact and a statement of fact.
2. In what three forms are statements about the fact usually made? What are the strengths and weaknesses of each?
3. What are the three common forms in which statements about the fact are used as supporting material?
4. What are the three main tests of induction?
5. How do we test deduction?
6. Distinguish between a proposition of judgment and a proposition of policy.
7. What are the two steps that are necessary in establishing a proposition of judgment?
8. What three steps are necessary in establishing a proposition of policy?

PROJECTS

1. Analyze the role of the reporter concerning facts in gathering material and writing a news story about a serious fire.
2. What went on at dinner last night? Be factual.
3. Why did you choose to attend this college? Which of your reasons had a logical basis? (This project, of course, can be only as successful as your honesty permits.)
4. Investigate the statistical basis on which national opinion polls or television rating organizations depend for their findings. Does their sampling system seem reasonable to you? What safeguards do they seem to try to take against getting a nonrepresentative sample?

MATERIAL FOR THOUGHT AND DISCUSSION

The modern "principle" is too often only a new form of an ancient taboo, rather than an enlightened rule of conduct. The person who justifies himself by saying that he holds certain beliefs, or acts in a manner "on principle," and yet refuses to examine the basis and expediency of his principle, introduces into his thinking and conduct an irrational, mystical element similar to that which characterized savage prohibitions. Principles unintelligently urged make a great deal of trouble in the free consideration of social adjustment, for they are frequently as recalcitrant and obscurantist as the primitive taboo, and are really scarcely more than an excuse for refusing to reconsider one's convictions and conduct. The pyschological conditions lying back of both taboo and this sort of principle are essentially the same. (*James Harvey Robinson,* The Mind in the Making. *New York: Harper & Row, 1939, p. 91.*)

❖❖❖❖

Mass movements do not usually rise until the prevailing order has been discredited. This discrediting is not an automatic result of the blunders and abuses of those in power, but the deliberate work of men of words with a grievance. Where the articulate are absent or without a grievance, the prevailing dispensation, though incompetent and corrupt, may continue in power until it falls and crumbles of itself. On the other hand, a dispensation of undoubted merit and vigor may be swept away if it fails to win the allegiance of the articulate minority. (*Eric Hoffer,* The True Believer. *New York: Harper & Row, 1962, p. 129.*)

We will never again understand nature as well as the Greek philosophers did. A general explanation of common phenomena in terms of a few all-embracing principles no longer satisfies us. We know too much. We must explain many things of which the Greeks were unaware. And, we require that our theories harmonize in detail with the very wide range of phenomena which they seek to explain. We insist that they provide us with useful guidance rather than rationalizations. (*J. R. Pierce,* Symbols, Signals and Noise. *New York: Harper & Row, 1961, p. 125.*)

Reference to Experience, as here used, means reference to the known. The known is that which the listener has seen, heard, read, felt, believed or done, and which still exists in his consciousness—his stock of knowledge. It embraces all those thoughts, feelings and happenings which are to him real. Reference to Experience, then, means *coming into the listener's life.*

Experiences may be resolved into two kinds—*Direct* and *Indirect.* Direct experiences include all those sensations, happenings, thoughts, that have been experienced by our own senses—what the ears have heard, the hands touched, the tongue tasted, the eyes seen, the mind thought. Indirect experiences include all those things which, while not felt or seen by ourselves, are accepted by us—knowledge second-hand. We never saw Julius Caesar, but we accept it as a reality that he lived and did certain things. We never saw Solomon's Temple, but we are sure that it once existed. Reference to Experience, therefore, means reference to those things which constitute our stock of knowledge, whether acquired directly or indirectly.

A moment's reflection will make clear the importance of this principle. What things are real to us? Of what things are we most positive? Those things which we have experienced. We know sugar is sweet, vinegar is sour, fire burns, because these things have actually given us those sensations. The certainty is born of our actual life, and if someone asserts the opposite we refuse to believe it. It is contrary to our experience. Our own experience, then, is the standard by which we test the truth or untruth of an assertion. Similarly, it is the means of making the unknown known. (*Arthur Edward Phillips,* Effective Speaking. *Chicago: The Newton Company, 1911, pp. 28–29.*)

❖❖❖❖

According to the most correct use of the term, a "Presumption" in favour of any supposition, means, not (as has been sometimes erroneously imagined) a preponderance of probability in its favour, but, such a *pre-occupation* of the ground, as implies that it must stand good till some sufficient reason is adduced against it; in short, that the *Burden of proof* lies on the side of him who would dispute it.

Thus, it is a well-known principle of the Law, that every man (including a prisoner brought up for trial) is to be *presumed* innocent till his guilt is established. This does not, of course, mean that we are to *take for granted* he is innocent; for if that were the case, he would be entitled to immediate liberation: nor does it mean that it is antecedently *more likely than not* that he is innocent; or, that the majority of these brought to trial are so. It evidently means only that the "burden of proof" lies with the accusers;—that he is not to be called on to prove his innocence, or to be dealt with as a criminal till he has done so; but that they are to bring their charges against him, which if he can repel, he stands acquitted.

Thus again, there is a "presumption" in favour of the right of any individuals or bodies-corporate to the property of which they are in *actual possession.* This does not mean that they are, or are not *likely* to be the rightful owners: but merely, that no man is to be disturbed in his possessions till some claim against him shall be established. He is not to be called on to prove his right; but the claimant, to disprove it; upon whom consequently the "burden of proof" lies. (*Richard Whately,* Elements of Rhetoric. *Louisville: Morton & Griswold, 1854, pp. 86–87.*)

❖❖❖❖

Whenever any publisher produces lessons specifically in the area of intergroup relations, they invariably turn out commendably for Jews, Catholics, and other groups. The . . . ambiguous images of other groups appear in lessons that have no intergroup purpose—which are intended to expound scripture or set forth doctrine. Positive efforts toward goodwill and understanding sometimes break down the moment one gets into *religious* teaching.

Why is this? Several reasons may be suggested. In writing lessons with a conscious intergroup interest, proper safeguards against prejudice are present: the writers chosen to write these lessons usually have achieved a certain competence in the field. The writer, furthermore, is put to studying something about the other group. He becomes conscious of his Christian obligation to love his neighbor and refrain from false witness against him. He is more sensitive to the requirements of justice, more disposed to look at empirical data, and to state the issues between groups profoundly and with a sense of fair play. But, when writing lessons the aim of which is to expound scripture or doctrine, other groups get mentioned marginally, incidentally, or unintentionally. Most intergroup references in each of the four curricula [studied by Olson] are of this nature. Because of their volume and accumulated impact they far outstrip in importance the carefully guarded statements found in intergroup lessons.

Often the negative writer is simply reminded of another group by some aspect of the scriptural passage he is handling. If this happens to be the doctrine of salvation by faith alone, for example, he may recall that the Roman Catholic Church challenges this doctrine. He judges the Catholic position false. The result is that when a number of writers in a curriculum do this, the aggregate image that emerges is that of a Roman Catholicism wholly unrelated to Protestantism and without a shred of truth in its teachings. Yet these same individual writers, if questioned as to their picture of Roman Catholicism, would hardly judge it a fair one. So one has the curious circumstance of a view of another group appearing in the materials that is at variance with the one that comes out in private conversation with writers and editors. *(Bernhard E. Olson, "Intergroup Relations in Protestant Teaching Materials,"* Religious Education. *New York: March–April 1960, pp. 135–136.)*

❖❖❖❖

It is necessary to consider separately these two hypotheses, each of which has a distinct branch of the argument corresponding to it. We can never be sure that the opinion we are endeavouring to stifle is a false opinion; and if we were sure, stifling it would be an evil still.

First: the opinion which it is attempted to suppress by authority may possibly be true. Those who desire to suppress it, of course deny its truth; but they are not infallible. They have no authority to decide the question for all mankind, and exclude every other person from the means of judging. To refuse a hearing to an opinion, because they are sure that it is false, is to assume that *their* certainty is the same thing as *absolute* certainty. All silencing of discussion is an assumption of infallibility. Its condemnation may be allowed to rest on this common argument, not the worse for being common. (*John Stuart Mill,* On Liberty, *1859.*)

9

Eloquence is vehement simplicity.—William Cecil

DELIVERY THAT ENHANCES THE SPOKEN WORD

A communication that is well organized, logical, fully supported, and adapted to the listener may still be unsuccessful if it is not presented in an interesting manner. A speaker who is listless, has a monotonous tone, talks too slowly or too fast, has distracting mannerisms, and shows no interest in his idea is almost bound to fail to achieve the desired response. Even communication in the informal atmosphere of the office, the club, the dormitory, or the committee meeting will lose clarity and impact with this kind of physical and vocal delivery. In more formal situations and before larger groups, poor delivery can lead to total ineffectiveness.

The question you may well ask, then, is, "What is a good style of delivery?" The first answer to this question is that there is no one style of presentation that fits each individual and each communication situation. The personalities that people project are too varied to permit one style of speaking to fit everyone. A low-key, intense style with limited but purposeful movement might be effective for one and inappropriate for another. A friendly, enthusiastic, and energetic style is suitable for some individuals and would distract the listener if attempted by others. In addition, the means of effective presentation vary from one situation to another. A delivery that would be effective with a large group might draw a negative reaction in a small, informal situation.

Each individual must become aware of his own methods of presentation and determine what manner interests and holds his listeners. His style of delivery must convey to the listeners his sincerity, his sense of urgency, or the importance of his idea. The listeners must feel that they are in direct contact with the speaker—that he is speaking with them, not at them.

Delivery must never be emphasized to the detriment of organization, support, or listener adaptation. Delivery is added to these factors to make the message of the speaker as clear and vital to the listener as possible. But let us discuss some specific items to which you can pay attention in analyzing your own delivery.

HOW TO ACHIEVE EFFECTIVE DELIVERY

You have a certain style of communication at present. You probably did not develop that style consciously; you have simply fallen into certain habits of vocal and physical delivery. Some of these are satisfactory; others detract from your communication. The first step in improving delivery is to study your present style in order to determine what you are doing that is all right and what needs elimination. Most of us are not conscious of what we do. We may have certain distracting mannerisms that we did not know about; we may not realize that our posture looks careless; we are not conscious of the fact that we seldom vary our pitch or rate of speaking.

The first step in improvement, then, is to determine what we are doing now. This can be done by self-analysis, with the aid of those around you. Class members and your instructor may assist; friends who watch you in various communication situations can help. Listen to yourself on a tape recorder if one is available; if your institution has a closed-circuit television set—with a video tape recorder, you can study both physical and vocal delivery. If you do use mechanical methods, record your speaking, not your reading, and have the recording made in as normal a situation as possible.

All of these means can help you to analyze your present delivery, but in the end improvement will depend on your own understanding of your problems and on whether you wish to do something about them. You may be told that you move too much, talk too fast, or fail to use variety, but until *you* hear these flaws or feel them yourself and decide to do something about them, little or no improvement will take place. Your present style has been developed by habit, and the portions of your delivery that are ineffective must be eliminated by substituting good habits for bad. When the good habits become a part of your style just as the old habits were, you will do the right things without thinking about it. However, each new habit must be established by practice, and that takes time, effort, and concentration.

The best time to work on establishing new habits is when you are at ease. Incorporate them into your delivery as you communicate in your room, in the dorm, and at club and committee meetings. It may take real conscious effort on your part, but in these informal situations you can make this effort and still not interfere with your communication.

ELIMINATING DISTRACTING HABITS IN DELIVERY

Physical and vocal delivery should never attract attention to itself and away from the idea being discussed. Here are a few examples of habits and mannerisms that can interfere with getting your point across:

Looking at the floor, at the ceiling, out the windows—anyplace but at the listeners
Speaking so rapidly that the listener gives up trying to follow the ideas
Speaking so slowly that the listener's attention can wander
Using unmotivated gestures (face-rubbing, ring-twisting, pencil-tapping) that attract the listener's eye

Constantly pacing back and forth or shifting weight from one foot to the other
Speaking in a dull, monotonous voice
Using so little facial expression that you appear to be uninterested in your own ideas
Standing or sitting in a posture that appears uncomfortable to your listeners

Activities like these will draw the conscious or unconscious attention of the listeners to your method of presentation. When this happens the listener can no longer be attentive to your idea and its development, and as a result he may fail to get your meaning, misunderstand what you are trying to say, or infer that you think the communication unimportant.

IMPROVING VOICE AND ACTION

The key words in improving delivery for more effective communication are variety and contrast. There is generally no such thing as utterance that is too fast or too slow, speech that is too loud or too soft, a pitch that is too high or too low. A problem develops when the voice is too *constantly* fast or slow, loud or soft, high or low. This is true also of physical activity. Too little or too much movement is seldom a problem in itself, but when a specific gesture is the only one used and it is used constantly, it calls attention to itself. In the same way, continued immobility appears awkward. Variety in physical and vocal activity is essential.

Contrast brings emphasis. If you have been talking loudly, a few quiet words will provide contrast, and your hearers will pay closer attention. The opposite is also true. If your rate of speech is suddenly slowed down, emphasis will be placed on the words uttered more slowly. Little physical movement followed by some definite action will tend to emphasize the words that accompany the change; immobility following considerable movement will tend to emphasize what is being said at that time. The purpose of contrast, then, is to emphasize the words being said at the time of the change.

Such change can help the speaker to bring out essential portions of his communication.

The whole body and voice must act as a unit during a presentation, but there are four aspects of delivery concerning which specific suggestions may be made. These are: (1) the eyes, (2) posture, (3) movement, and (4) the voice.

The eyes

One of the important goals of delivery is to make the listener feel that he is part of the communication. The eyes play an important part in achieving this goal. The speaker must look at his listener or listeners and make them feel that he is talking to them. If he is constantly looking at notes, at the floor, out the window, or in some other direction, he interferes with his communication in two ways. First, the listener is likely to distrust the motives of the man who does not look him in the eye. At best, it seems that the speaker is not very interested in his message or in the listener; at worst, he might seem dishonest. To be thought "shifty-eyed" is not desirable. Second, when the speaker looks out the window or at the floor, listeners are likely to wonder what he sees there. Some people might try to follow his gaze, and their attention will wander away from him and what he is saying. Refusal to look at the audience is basically a nervous habit, and should be overcome rather than allowed to interfere with communication.

Posture

The position that a speaker assumes, either seated or standing, is also important in communication. Proper posture will show two things: (1) that you are in control of yourself during the communication, and (2) that you have a real interest in what you are saying. Sloppy posture will create the impression, true or false, that you are nervous or do not really care what happens. The listener unconsciously gets cues from looking at you, and if these cues tell him that you are not sure of yourself or that you have little interest in what you are saying, he may decide that you are not worth hearing. There are few hard and fast rules about what posture helps to get ideas across. It is possible to appear at ease and alert while seated, speaking from behind a rostrum, or resting one hand on a table; but if you slouch, drape yourself awkwardly on the rostrum, or lean clumsily on one arm, these same postures can detract from your effectiveness. This point is illustrated in even the most informal of conversational situations—a bull session at the dorm, for instance, with the participants draped in various attitudes over the furniture, or even stretched out on the floor. The negligence of posture (and eye contact) that commonly obtains in such settings reflects the feeling of the participants that nothing of much importance is being said. But let the conversation touch on a topic of real concern to one or more of the members, and there will be a notable change in alertness of posture and an attempt to include the whole group in the communication. When idle conversation is replaced with intent to obtain a discriminatory response, the physical attitude of the communicator reflects the change.

There is no single way to stand or sit to create a good impression. Your posture should (1) be comfortable for you, (2) look comfortable to your listeners, and most important, (3) create an impression of interest in the topic and a desire to communicate. Any posture that accomplishes these goals is satisfactory.

Gesture

A posture that achieves the goals established in the previous paragraph forms a good basis on which to build good body movement. One aspect of this movement is the use of the hands. Proper movement of the hands can add to the impact of the presentation; gestures can assist in getting emphasis, in signifying various points of the speech, in showing divisions in the communication, and in making comparisons of ideas. Action of this nature makes the speaker a more interesting individual to watch and thus listener interest can be maintained. Besides, most people use gestures in conversation. Suppressing these natural movements usually results in awkwardness.

One caution should be issued here. Gestures should have some purpose and meaning. If the movement of the hands is constant and random, having little to do with the presentation, it will hinder effectiveness. By the same token, a constant repetition of the same hand movement is distracting and harmful to successful communication.

Body movement

Movement of the whole body can aid the impact of the presentation. A shift in posture or even moving to another place between ideas will assist the listener to recognize divisions within the communication. A step forward can bring the listener closer in a psychological sense for better interaction, and so make him more receptive to an important idea. Movement can change the background behind the speaker slightly so that the listener will not become tired of looking at the same view for too long. Again, be sure that the movement is not merely random wandering, but has some purpose and control behind it.

A further purpose is served by body movement of this type as well as by gestures: it gives the communicator an opportunity to release some of his nervous tension.

Vocal variety

We all have within us the physical potential to use our voices well. In fact, even the speaker with the most monotonous voice will use variety when he is angry or particularly excited. As we have said before, the reason for monotony is habit. Some individuals have developed the habit of no variety, or too fast or slow a pace. Others feel that they must never pause, and so fill the gaps with "uh" or "and-uh". These habits may be so strong that drastic means must be used to break them. For instance, an instructor may ask a class to count aloud when a speaker uses "uh" or "and-uh" for a vocalized pause. Usually the speaker will stop using the expression after the listeners have counted to four or five.

As we said at the beginning of this chapter, there is no one style of delivery that fits every person. Each individual must adopt a style that suits his own personality and the situation in which he finds himself. The comments presented above are merely guideposts to help each person analyze his own style, correct those things that get in the way of effectiveness, and add those attributes that will help with the impact and clarity of the communication.

VISUAL MATERIAL

The delivery of a presentation may be greatly enhanced by the use of visual material. Seeing as well as hearing during a communication may help in one or all of three ways: (1) achieving greater clarity and comprehension, (2) creating and maintaining interest during the communication, and (3) helping the listener to remember important material that is presented.

To achieve clarity

As was pointed out in an earlier chapter, we should use as many channels of communication as we need to get an idea across to listeners. This means that on occasions the use of the visual channel can be of real value. The use of the chalkboard or a sheet of paper on which a difficult definition is written can give the listener an additional opportunity for concentration and understanding. Figures, particularly in quantity, are more readily comprehended when seen than when heard. Comparisons shown by bar graphs may achieve in seconds what it would take minutes to explain orally. A picture or drawing may show relationships almost impossible to explain orally. These examples are just a few of the myriad possibilities of how visual material may bring to the communication situation a clarity not attainable by words alone. The speaker must consider before beginning his communication how best to achieve his goal. If visual aids are desirable for clarity they should be employed.

To gain and hold interest

At times it is important for a speaker to use visual materials even though they are not basically essential for clarity. The opportunity to view as well as listen may increase the listener's interest and attention. Television has many more viewers than radio has listeners because it allows one to see as well as hear. On occasions, seeing something may lead to better comprehension, but often it is simply more interesting when we have something to watch.

A speech on high school drop-outs might be understood clearly in a presentation by words alone. However, if you show figures on how many students drop out, what they do after leaving school, the comparison of the income of drop-outs with that of those who finish, and the cost of crime and welfare, the communication may be more interesting and have a greater impact. Some of the visuals may help understanding, but they are mostly for interest.

To help the listener to remember the communication

Our discussion of the purpose of oral communication pointed out that since the actual response to a communication is often delayed, it is important for the listener to remember as much as possible about the presentation. Visual material can help greatly in achieving this goal. One research study that compared the recall of a speech that was read, a spoken presentation, and a spoken presentation with visual aids pointed out that the last method was twice as effective as a speech without visual aids in securing delayed recall of the speech.[1] The implanting of certain words, figures, comparisons, or ideas can often be done better by visual means or by a combination of visual and oral devices.

TYPES OF VISUAL MATERIAL

We may often think of visuals as the artistic and costly material painted by commercial artists. This type of aid certainly plays a part in communication, but simple aids made by the speaker can be just as effective. If the group is small, simple words, figures, or drawings on a piece of posterboard that can be seen by all will accomplish our goal. These can be produced during the presentation or may be prepared before the communication. For larger groups, a neat printing or drawing on a handy piece of cardboard may be effective. The chalkboard or flip-charts may be used, or a simple handout that the listeners may use individually may bring excellent results.

For more formal situations with larger audiences, it may be desirable to use a mechanical means of production. Drawings on acetate cards may be enlarged by the use of an overhead projector. These drawings may be done as the speech progresses, or may be prepared in advance. Slide projectors and flannel-boards may be used to good advantage in situations where there is ample time for preparation of material before the speech.

The important idea is that the communicator take the time to determine how he can best achieve the response he seeks. In many instances, this will require the use of some visuals. Determining the type of visual to be used is not so important as determining whether any type of visual presentation would aid the effectiveness of the presentation.

[1] Franklin H. Knower, David Phillips, and Fern Koeppel, "Studies in Listening to Informative Speaking," *Journal of Abnormal and Social Psychology* (January 1945), pp. 203–213.

CAUTIONS CONCERNING VISUALS

Visual presentations often fail because certain considerations were not taken into account. The main reasons for errors are: (1) the size of the visual is not adequate, (2) the visual contains too much material, (3) the visual apparently gives away the essence of the speech, (4) the visual is sloppily or inaccurately prepared, and (5) the meaning of the visual is not immediately clear to the listener.

Size

The speaker often forgets to consider his listeners when making a visual aid. The words that he writes or the drawing that he makes on a paper or a chalkboard must be large enough to be clear to all viewers. A picture or drawing in a book could be used as an integral part of the communication, but only a few listeners can see the details. The speaker who makes a visual ahead of time, or even during the presentation, may fail because he can easily view what he is drawing and he therefore assumes that everyone else can do so too. A visual not large enough to be seen will not only destroy the effectiveness of the point concerned, but may lose the listener for everything that follows.

Content

The speaker may use a map, chart, graph, drawing, or picture that contains what he wants, but also contains many other things that are not essential to the presentation. The listener may find it difficult to separate the essentials from the nonessentials, or he may become so interested in minor aspects of the visual that he does not concentrate on the needed portion and thus misses the point being made. It may be necessary for the speaker to copy a portion of a visual that he needs, leaving out the extraneous material. Only information that is necessary and relevant should be shown to an audience.

Clues to the essence of the speech

Some speakers make the mistake of putting all the information for a whole communication into one visual. The listeners can view what is coming, and their curiosity will carry them forward instead of following what the speaker is concentrating on at the moment. Visuals that seem to move forward with the presentation are better. A separate aid can be made for each idea to be visualized, or material to be discussed later can be covered until ready for use. By this method, the speaker can hold the concentration of his listeners where he desires at any given time. The previous visuals can be shown for comparison or contrast, or to jog the memory.

Neatness

A visual that looks hurried or sloppy can affect the listener negatively. This is one of the problems of the use of the chalkboard. Unless carefully planned, use of the board as you speak can create the impression of confusion and carelessness. The visual presentation need not be highly artistic, but it should be neatly done.

Comprehensibility

A visual that is complex and not immediately clear may confuse the listener. If it is necessary to use two or more visuals concentrating on various aspects of what is being presented, do so and then combine them at the end. Or the use of color can help to make your presentation clearer. In a diagram showing how an automobile operates, the ignition system could be shown in one color, the fuel distribution system in a second, and the braking system in a third. In advocating a change in the organization of student government, you might use a chart showing the current plan in blue, additions that you advocate in yellow, and elements to be eliminated in red.

CONCLUSION

Physical delivery of a speech—the management of voice and bodily activity—must be adapted to the style of the individual speaker. There is no one style that ought to be followed by everyone. To insure making the most effective use of delivery, you must first become aware of the style that you have thus far unconsciously developed; analysis will suggest elements that should be improved upon.

Distracting mannerisms should be eliminated. Good eye contact helps to make the listeners feel a part of the communication. Posture should both feel and look comfortable, and give the impression of alertness and interest in the message. Most of us naturally gesture during much of our communication; only occasionally do these gestures call attention to themselves. An artificial rigidity, by which a speaker attempts to avoid gesturing, soon looks awkward and uncomfortable. Movement can be purposeful and so aid the communication; random or excessive movement betrays nervousness and interferes with communication. Vocal variety is important in speaking, and habitual use of vocalized pauses interferes with the effect of a message.

Visual materials that are well chosen and well handled may help to achieve clarity, gain and hold interest, or strengthen the recall of the listener. A wide variety of visuals are available for use with various kinds of audiences. Visual materials should be large enough to be seen and simple, clear, and neat enough to be understood; a good visual does not make the communication by itself.

REVIEW QUESTIONS

1. What is the first step in improving the delivery of your communication?
2. List at least five distracting mannerisms that detract from attention to the ideas expressed.

3. What is the main attribute of good vocal delivery?
4. What effect has poor eye contact on one's listeners?
5. What constitutes good posture?
6. Under what circumstances is it incorrect to use gestures?
7. What three purposes may the use of visual aids serve in communication?
8. What are the common errors in making use of visuals?

PROJECTS

1. Do the physical and/or vocal aspects of certain students in your dormitory have anything to do with your liking or respect for them? Explain.
2. Rate your instructors in order of their effectiveness as lecturers. Now rate them on their physical and vocal delivery. Any relationship?

MATERIAL FOR THOUGHT AND DISCUSSION

Of all the qualities above mentioned, the first and most essential is perspicuity [clarity]. Every speaker doth not propose to please the imagination, nor is every subject susceptible of those ornaments which conduce to this purpose. Much less is it the aim of every speech to agitate the passions. There are some occasions, therefore, on which vivacity, and many on which animation of style, are not necessary; nay, there are occasions on which the last especially would be improper. But whatever be the ultimate intention of the orator, to inform, to convince, to please, to move, or to persuade, still he must speak so as to be understood, or he speaks to no purpose. If he does not propose to convey certain sentiments into the minds of his hearers by the aid of signs intelligible to them, he may as well declaim before them in an unknown tongue. . . .

There is another difference also between perspicuity and the last two mentioned qualities, vivacity and animation, which deserves to be remarked. In a discourse wherein either or both of these is requisite, it is not every sentence that requires, or even admits them;

but every sentence ought to be perspicuous. The effect of all the other qualities of style is lost without this. This being to the understanding what light is to the eye, ought to be diffused over the whole performance. (*George Campbell,* The Philosophy of Rhetoric. *London: W. Strahan and T. Cadell, 1776, Vol. 2, pp. 5–6.*)

❖❖❖❖

Though action may seem to be merely in the eye, the hand, or the face, it really has, when genuine, a subtle connection with the whole body. The eye and face lead and govern the action of the other parts of the body. From these the emotion sweeps over the body like a wave, and all parts become consistent with the activity at the centre.

Without unity there can be no art. Unity in action can be secured only by genuineness of realization. The imagination and the sympathies must be awakened. The student must speak with his whole nature. Expression must not be merely local or one-sided. It must be the living utterance of a living man. A normal organism is alive in every part. It is this that makes action so important. It expresses the real life, and will forever be the deepest witness of genuineness.

The natural languages seem far apart at first. Modulations of the voice are addressed to the ear; action of the body to the eye. Their functions being distinct, many think that action need not always be present and that it is purely accidental. This is a serious mistake. Practically no true, expressive tone, no complete expression is possible without action. (*S. S. Curry,* Foundations of Expression. *Boston: The Expression Company, 1907, p. 275.*)

❖❖❖❖

(*At one time it was believed that pauses and punctuation were related.*)

A Comma stops the Voice while we may privately tell *one,* a Simicolon *two;* a Colon *three:* and a Period *four.* . . . But besides these, there are four more Notes or Distinctions of Pause, viz. a Parenthesis; which requires the Pause of a *Comma* at least, and sometimes a Simi-colon after it. 2. a *Double-Period,* or Blank Line, (–); which denotes the Pause of two Periods, or half a Paragraph. 3. *A Paragraph* or *Break;* when the Line is broke or left imperfect, and the next begins under the second or third Letter of the preceding Line; and denotes the Pause of two double Periods. 4. A double *Paragraph,* that is, when the next Line not only begins shorter than the preceding, but leaves the Space of a whole Line vacant between them; which shews that the Voice is to rest during the Time of two Paragraphs [or while we "privately tell" thirty-two!]. ([*John Mason,*] An Essay on Elocution. *London: M. Cooper, 1748, pp. 22, 21.*)

When however I protest against all artificial systems of Elocution, and all *direct* attention to Delivery, *at the time,* it must not be supposed that a *general* inattention to that point is recommended; or that the most perfect Elocution is to be attained by never thinking at all on the subject; though it may safely be affirmed that even this negative plan would succeed far better than a studied modulation. But it is evident that if any one wishes to *assume the Speaker* as far as possible, *i.e.* to deliver a written composition with some degree of the manner and effect of one that is extemporaneous, he will have a considerable difficulty to surmount: since though this may be called, in a certain sense, the Natural Manner, it is far from being what he will naturally, *i.e., spontaneously,* fall into. It is by no means natural for anyone to *read* as if he were *not* reading, but speaking. And again, even when anyone is reading what he does not wish to deliver as his own composition, . . . it is evident that this may be done better or worse, in infinite degrees; and that though (according to the views here taken) a studied attention to the sounds uttered, at the time of uttering them, leads to an affected and offensive delivery, yet, on the other hand, an utterly careless reader cannot be a good one. (*Richard Whately,* Elements of Rhetoric. *Louisville: Morton & Griswold, 1854, p. 239.*)

We must not fail to notice that each kind of rhetoric has its own appropriate style. The style of written prose is not the same as that of controversial speaking; nor, in the latter, is the style of public discussion the same as that of the law-courts. A knowledge of both the written and the spoken style is required. . . . The written [literary] style is the more finished; the controversial is far better adapted to dramatic delivery, whether for the kind of speaking that reflects character, or the emotional kind. . . . On comparison, speeches of the literary men sound thin in the actual contests; while those of the orators sound well, but look crude when you have them in your hands—and the reason is that their place is in a contest. (*Lane Cooper,* The Rhetoric of Aristotle. *New York: Appleton-Century-Crofts, 1932, p. 127.*)[2]

[2] Reprinted by permission of Appleton-Century-Crofts.

10

"When I use a word," Humpty Dumpty said, in rather a scornful tone, "it means just what I choose it to mean—neither more nor less."—Lewis Carroll, Through the Looking Glass

THE LANGUAGE OF COMMUNICATION

If someone were to ask you, "What is a word?" you would probably reply by saying something about how we use words. "A word," you might say, "is the smallest unit of a language." Or perhaps you would say that a word is a symbol for an idea. Although these typical attempts at definition tell us something about words, they also typically leave out an element that—once you are told—may seem both too obvious and too trivial to merit attention: words are *things, objects, natural phenomena,* like chairs, smoke, rivers, and thunder. The words you are now reading actually consist of color patches on a base; so do Van Gogh's *Sunflowers* and the oil spots on the floor of your garage. Spoken words are patterns of rarefaction and compaction of air molecules, like the wail of a siren, the rustling of leaves, or a performance of a symphony. Words may be pieces of bent glass tubing filled with neon gas, indentations incised into tombstones or public buildings, or thin strips of icing squeezed out on a cake. What we are trying to say is that words have a physical existence. Some of our problems with language arise from our attempts to use words without recognizing what they are.

These physical entities that we call words function as symbols, just as traffic lights, pink or blue bootees, a clenched fist shaken under your nose, or an Eagle Scout badge. That is to say, they are not important to us for what they themselves are—bits of glass, metal, yarn, ribbon, skin and bones. Their significance lies in the things they stand for or symbolize. In this chapter we shall consider the ways in which words can symbolize other things, or acquire meanings; and how those meanings may be communicated to others.

WHAT WORDS MEAN

These noises and marks by which we communicate ideas are special kinds of noises and marks, of course. They are useful to us because they convey meaning. Now let us examine the nature of that meaning.

Suppose that you are working on your car, and need another tool. You may say to a friend who is helping you, "Hand me that thing on the bench there," or you may say, "Give me that 5/8″ crescent wrench." In both cases you know what it is that you are asking someone else to do. But one request is much more likely than the other to produce the desired response. There are two reasons why this is so: one has to do with the difference between public and private meanings, and the other with levels of abstraction.

Public and private meanings

When any of us uses a word, it means, as Humpty Dumpty pointed out to Alice, precisely what he intends it to mean—for him. The question for communication is, what does the word mean to our listeners? Any word has a cluster of meanings, and we can divide these into two groups. First there are the public meanings of the word—what everyone means when he uses the word. The second are the private meanings of the word—those ideas that are added by the user (either speaker or hearer) in this particular occurrence of the word.

When we analyze the significance of these definitions, we discover that the public meanings of many words are very restricted. What is a chair, for instance? We would all agree, probably, that it is a piece of furniture, with a back, designed for one person to sit on. But an individual using the word "chair" may have in mind as his private meaning anything from a hard, wooden folding chair to a big, well-upholstered reclining chair. The important thing to remember for communication is that the listeners will not know what private meanings the speaker had in mind; they will supply their own private meanings when they hear a word. When you asked your friend for "that thing on the bench," your meaning for "thing" was quite clear in your own mind: you meant the 5/8" crescent wrench. But the public meaning of the word "thing"—and that is all you can be sure of communicating—is so vague and general that your friend would probably have no idea at all of what you were talking about unless he had some clues beyond your use of the language.

Level of abstraction

The reason that the word "thing" must depend almost entirely on private meanings or other cues if it is to convey much meaning is that it is one of the most abstract words we have. Now let us see what that statement means.

We ordinarily think of abstract words as those whose meanings are vague, general, hard to put a finger on. Concrete words, on the other hand, are more tangible—we can see, hear, feel the things to which they refer. But it is very difficult to divide words into two clear classes—abstract and concrete. We find that there is a long continuum, with some words more or less abstract or concrete than others. Let us look into the derivation of the word "abstract" to see why this is so.

To abstract is to separate or draw something out—the

abstract of an article "draws out" and summarizes the main ideas of the author. Paradoxically, the more abstract our language is, the less it "draws out" of (or says about) the thing in the world to which it is referring. The alternative term we suggest for "thing" in the previous section is at a very low level of abstraction. "That 5/8″ crescent wrench" describes rather specifically the object that you are naming. Let us start at this low level of abstraction and go several levels higher to see how each successive level leaves out more and more of what might be said about the actual object in the world, and leaves the significance more and more up to the private meanings of the listener.

If you were merely to ask for a crescent wrench, you might be handed one too small or too large for the use you had for it. At the next level, had you only requested a *wrench,* you might have got any one of a number of kinds: pipe, monkey, end, etc. Had you asked for a *tool,* the public meaning of this word is only what the wrench you want has in common with hammers, pliers, screwdrivers, and saws. By the time we get to this level, it should be clear that the word "tool" really says very little about the actual wrench that you need—it abstracts from the object itself only the capability of being used to do some work. *Hardware* is even more abstract; *equipment* includes a good deal besides hardware. By the time we work our way up to a highly abstract word like "thing," we are saying so little about whatever we are referring to that we must rely largely on cues other than the word itself to get any meaning from it at all.

In communication, therefore, it is important that the speaker remember in choosing his language that words—the noises that he is going to make—will not automatically convey the private meanings that he assigns to them; they will convey only the public meanings of those words, and will stir up in his hearers *their* private meanings. The more abstract the language of a communication, the less public meaning it conveys, and the more it relies on the private meanings of the hearers. Therefore the careful speaker will make his language as concrete as possible—will stick to words at the lower levels of abstraction, and will constantly ask himself, "What will my listeners understand when I say this?"

HOW WORDS ACQUIRE MEANINGS

Words acquire meanings through experience. We learn the names of relatives and friends of the family, of colors and letters and numbers, of household objects, as someone points to the object and makes a certain noise. As our experiences and vocabularies grow, it becomes possible for us to learn meanings by asking for definitions—that is, we ask what words may be used in the place of a word that we do not understand. But if a definition is to be of any help to us, it must be expressed in terms that we do understand—that we can relate back to our own experience.

The importance of experience in learning is emphasized by laboratory courses in which hundreds of students perform the same experiment in the same way, most of the time knowing in advance exactly what the result will be. We read our textbooks with much greater comprehension after having dissected our own frogs or experimented with various pendulums ourselves. The graduate student in education who has taught for a couple of years before returning to his studies will read with quite a different kind of understanding from that of the student who has gone straight from undergraduate training to graduate work without any teaching experience.

Our attitudes also color the meanings that we attach to words. A tourist who had just returned from a trip through some of the most breath-taking scenery of the far West was asked about her travels. "It was just mountains," she replied. A person who is insensitive to a topic, or who is emotionally involved either for or against it, is likely to find his attitude coloring the meanings of words that deal with the topic.

The speaker then, must recognize that the private meanings his hearers will attach to the words that he uses will be based on their experience and attitudes unless he makes very clear to them what he is trying to convey. Much of the time we communicate with people of similar background and experience; the fact that this is commonly true may blind us to the necessity for adapting our language to the backgrounds of our hearers on those occasions when this is necessary.

HOW WORDS CONVEY MEANINGS

The central admonition that this chapter should carry to the reader who is really interested in communication is this: The meaning that a word conveys to a listener or reader is the meaning that *he* attaches to it, not the meaning that the communicator intends to convey. Meanings are in *people,* not in *words;* words are only the "sticks" with which we try to stir up in the mind of the listener some meaning that is appropriate to our purpose in communicating.

It should become immediately apparent, then, that the only meaning that we can count on conveying by means of a word is its public meaning—and the public meaning says very little about the thing to which it refers. We must remember that our private meanings do not go along with the word when we speak it; the word merely picks up whatever meanings the listener attaches to it.

We do, however, manage much of the time to communicate with reasonable effectiveness. Part of the reason is that meanings are frequently suggested by the context of an utterance.

Part of the context is physical. We pick up many ideas concerning what a speaker means by watching him. His posture, facial expression, and gestures give us some clues. Tone of voice tells us much about the meaning that the speaker is trying to convey. This is one reason why talking to others is much more satisfactory than writing notes. Although we may use capitals, italics, underlining, punctuation marks, and other typographical devices to try to convey the tone of a message, most of them are only partially satisfactory. An imaginative recognition of the importance of the tone of voice is seen in Walt Kelly's *Pogo.* The Deacon in this comic strip always speaks in Old English script, P. T. Bridgeport speaks in circus poster typography, and Sarcophagus MacAbre's comments are placed in "balloons" with heavy black borders.

We get contextual clues as well from the general subject matter. Perhaps you run across a word now and then that you have never seen before, and still you do not bother to look it up in a dictionary. You may be able to guess at the meaning of the word because of the subject that is being discussed, or even because of the way in which it is used in the sentence. The psychological context can also moderate the meaning of language. "Horsethief," "fink," and even more opprobrious words may be terms of respect, and even affection, under certain circumstances.

Although contexts can give us considerable assistance in getting our meanings across, we cannot overemphasize the point that it is the meanings attached to a word by the listener that determine its signification for him.

CONCLUSION

It is not enough for a speaker to say what he means—to express himself well. He must stir up in the minds of his hearers the ideas that he wants to convey. The main tools for accomplishing this objective are words. But since we are so accustomed to using words, we are likely to overlook the fact that they can sometimes be barriers to effective communication, and that there are methods by which we can use words to serve our communications better.

The speaker must remember that words are merely noises that he makes, and that the meanings that they acquire reflect the experience and attitudes of those who use them. He should therefore endeavor to use words that are as concrete and specific as possible in order to rely less on private meanings.

REVIEW QUESTIONS

1. What is a word? What is a symbol?
2. Distinguish between the public meanings and your private meanings for the word "school."
3. Arrange the following words in order of abstraction levels, from the lowest to the highest: bird, living creature, thrush, vertebrate, robin.
4. How do words acquire meanings?
5. Specify some of the contexts within which you understand the meaning of this sentence.
6. Explain why words do not convey meanings, but only stir them up.

PROJECTS

1. Choose a simple, common, everyday word like "house," "tree," "book," or "street." Watch for occurrences of the word in communication going on about you. Write out in detail the meanings that you think the speakers intended to convey by the use of the word.
2. Analyze some of the problems that may arise in discussing with your parents your school work or a job that you have held. To what extent is their ability or inability to attach the same meanings to some of your words responsible for the problem?
3. During the informal discussion of a topic of interest, pick a word that recurs and try to analyze the different meanings of the word in the minds of different listeners—or even how one person uses the word to mean different things at different times.
4. Compare and contrast the language in which men and women discuss the latest fashions, automobiles, a prominent politician. Account for the differences.
5. Describe several contexts in which you might hear the expression, "Yes, dear!" Show how the meanings vary, often drastically.

MATERIAL FOR THOUGHT AND DISCUSSION

In some cases, sights, sounds, tastes, feels, and smells, are presented to us disjunctively. One sight, which is thus presented to us, we call moon. Another sight we call light; and another, aurora borealis, meteor, ignis fatuus, etc. A certain unassociated feel, we call air. Another feel, we call wind; and another, cold. A certain unassociated sound, we call echo. Thunder can hardly be designated as an unassociated sound, for it is usually associated with a sight which we call lightning. Tastes and smells are never presented to us, unless in association with some other existence. I recall only one exception, and we designate it, when it occurs, by saying, we have an unpleasant taste in our mouths. . . .

The number of unassociated sights is very small, if we estimate them by the number of words which name such sights. They are, however, far more numerous than this mode of estimating them will imply. The word star, for instance, names an unassociated sight, (a sight not associated with any feel, etc.;) but the word which thus seems to name but one sight, names a great number of sights, that differ in magnitude, brilliancy, colour, shape, etc. I state this, to enable you to perceive, that verbal designations are an inadequate means of estimating the variety and number of natural existences.

The sights which are presented to us in association with feels, etc., are also far more numerous and various than language implies. Colours alone are almost infinite in variety, while our names for them are comparatively a few words. But a large portion of sights we never attempt to designate by specifick appelations. When I look at a chair, I discern a different sight from what I see when I look at fire; still, for the sight alone of neither the chair nor the fire, language possesses no name. The words chair and fire apply severally to an associated sight and feel. When we speak of the sight alone, we employ a periphrasis, and say the appearance of fire, the appearance of chair, etc. . . .

Men have been more sparing of names to tastes, smells, sounds, and feels, than even to sights. Fragrant, fetid, and a few other words, are all that we have deigned to appropriate to the information of the sense of smelling. Hot, cold, pain, etc., are all which we have appropriated to specifick feels, though nature presents them to us in boundless variety. When I touch iron, I realize a different feel from what I experience when I touch wood, silk, wool, linen, etc; but to none of these feels is a name appropriated. The word iron names an associated sight and feel. The same may be said of the words wood, silk, wool, linen, etc. . . .

But not only numerous sights, sounds, tastes, feels, and smells, possess separately no name; many associations of them possess no name. We name such associations only as utility requires us to designate. A certain associated sight and feel we designate by the word square, and others we name round, flat, etc.; but a hundred shapes which may be assumed by a piece of glass, on its accidental fracture, we have not designated by any name. *(Alexander Bryan Johnson,* A Treatise on Language, *ed. by David Rynin. Berkeley: University of California Press, 1959, pp. 49–50. Johnson's treatise was originally printed in 1836.)*

The problems of the executive in this field are difficult. He must necessarily deal on a fairly high level of abstraction because he cannot know the particular individuals or the particular problems they face in the work situation. The executive is too many levels of authority above the shop for such detailed knowledge. He cannot operate at all unless his information is generalized and abstracted.

This is well illustrated in the field of accounting. Figures on labor costs, wages, and all other cost items for a particular plant or department of a plant can readily be transmitted to the top executive of the company. Such figures can be misleading in various ways, but at least they do present something of a general and abstract picture of the situation which the executive can use in his thinking and planning.

In the field of industrial relations, the executive also deals in high level abstractions, but these abstractions, in contrast to those in accounting, tend to be quite divorced from the actual work situations. The figures on production or labor costs can readily be checked back to the plant for additional information or interpretation. Not so with the prevalent abstractions in the field of industrial relations. In that field there tends to be a tremendous unfilled chasm between the abstractions used by the executive in thinking about his problems and the actual problems as they are experienced in the factory. In order to "make sense"—in order to relate language to action—the executive needs to be able to talk up and down the ladder of abstraction. He must be able to connect low level abstraction . . . with high level abstractions. For this purpose we desperately need a new set of symbols, a language of human relations in industry. It is one of the tasks of research men in this field to develop such a set of symbols. Already we feel this task is far advanced. We can observe a particular problem situation in a factory and translate it into abstract terms so that the executive can look upon a problem of organization without having to know all there is to know about the particular individuals involved. As this language becomes better known and more skillfully applied, it will be possible to make greater progress in the stormy area of industrial relations. (*William Foote Whyte, "Semantics and Industrial Relations,"* Human Organization, *Spring 1949, p. 10. Society for Applied Anthropology.*)

11

The sheer act of listening may itself be far more persuasive than anything we might have to say—and there is a strong possibility we might learn something we didn't know before.—Editors of Fortune[1]

LISTENING AS AN EFFECTIVE TOOL IN COMMUNICATION

Aristotle's *Rhetoric* is the earliest speech text that has survived intact, but we know that even before his time men were concerned about the principles that could be employed to make a person a more effective speaker. It has been only in recent years, however, that there has been a recognition of the need for training in methods of effective listening. It has been recognized by all writers in the field of speech that the speaker must give proper consideration to his listeners. However, few rhetoricians have discussed the methods that a listener might employ to catch the full impact of any communication.

The communication models that have been developed recently, like the one discussed in Chapter 3, have placed renewed stress on the fact that the speaker and listener are constantly changing places. This emphasis on the interaction of the speaker and listener has opened up new ideas relative to the communication situation, and has given impetus to the study of the listener's role.

1 "Is Anybody Listening?" *Fortune* (September 1950), p. 83.

Some recent research shows that learning to listen and gaining an understanding of the role of the listener can aid us in remembering for a longer time more of what has been said in a communication situation.

The quickest way for a student to see how differently people listen is to compare notes with another member of a lecture class. One student is certain to discover that he has noted down things that the other did not, and vice versa. Even what are listed as the important ideas of the lecture may vary from student to student, and the amount of detail will vary even more. Any teacher who has collected the notes of his students to see what they learned from a given lecture wonders if the students are in the same class or even in the same course.

The ability of a student to listen effectively will play an important role in his success in college. The ability of a manager to listen well may have considerable influence on his future in a company. Good listening by the doctor, the lawyer, the engineer, the social worker, and others saves considerable time, reduces misconceptions, and even avoids serious errors.

Let us divide our discussion of listening into two major areas: (1) the human static that tends to block good listening, and (2) the development of a method of listening well.

HUMAN STATIC

We are all familiar with the electrical static that on occasion makes listening to the radio difficult if not impossible. We know that this static can blot out words or phrases that are essential to the meaning of what is being said. If the static is so bad that listening becomes too difficult, we either turn the radio off or switch to another station. The same thing happens in a face-to-face communication situation, but this time the source of the static is not electrical but human. We know that certain things may happen that block true comprehension and at times cause us to "tune out" altogether. An examination of some of the more important elements of human static may be valuable.

Preconceived notions

You may be familiar with the story of the young Mexican boy, Miguel, who rode his bicycle up to the Texas border with two large bags of sand slung over his shoulders. The border patrol was fairly sure that Miguel was smuggling something into the United States, so they took the bags from his shoulders and examined them carefully. They found nothing but sand in the bags. Two weeks later, when the same event occurred, they took the bags off, dumped the contents on the floor, and examined the sand almost grain by grain. They were unsuccessful in finding any contraband. After six months of unsuccessful searches, the head of the border patrol was about to retire. He took Miguel aside and promised no prosecution if the Mexican lad would tell him what he was smuggling. Miguel blandly answered, "Bicycles." Preconceived notions about smuggling techniques had made the patrolmen miss the obvious.

An art professor in a major university reports that in the first course in art much of the teacher's time must be spent overcoming his students' preconceived notions of what art is. Only then can real learning take place. Many industrial companies hold what are called "brainstorming sessions." During these sessions no one is allowed to evaluate or refute any suggestion that is made, and suggestions of any nature concerning the problem at hand are encouraged. The main reason for these sessions is that many of the plant meetings and committee sessions are so full of preconceived notions that new ideas die aborning. Medical researchers for years had been aware of the mould that "ruined" many of their specimens. It was not until Sir Alexander Fleming looked at mould from a different point of view that penicillin was discovered.

New ideas, new approaches to problems, and new solutions to old troubles often have a difficult time receiving a proper hearing. Many listeners do not really listen; they place certain interpretations on early words or suggestions and conclude that the speaker's idea will not work. They fail to listen to the whole idea, study it, and then determine whether it is worthwhile or not. They come to their conclusions immediately on the basis of preconceived notions rather than on an evaluation of the speaker's presentation.

Students in classes are often guilty of this behavior. Because of preconceived notions, they assume that what is being said at a certain time is not of value to them, or that it is a rehash of what they already know. They fail to listen attentively, and as a result miss significant facts, or fail to see a new approach to the topic under discussion. The time to determine whether a lecture offers anything new is after the lecture is over, not early in the class period.

Prejudice

Closely related to the human static of preconceived notions is the barrier to good listening called prejudice. With prejudice in the way, we are not hearing the idea so much as we are hearing the person who says it. Good ideas may come from people whom we do not like; conversely, poor ideas can come from people we respect.

As we saw in our discussion in Chapter 5, listeners undoubtedly give better attention and more belief to people who have won their respect. However, we should not evaluate an idea mainly on the basis of who said it; we should base our judgments on the explanation or support that is presented.

The judgment is made *after* the communication; we should not conclude that an idea is worthwhile or unworthy merely on the basis of our feelings about the person who expresses it.

The most common prejudices are with regard to race, color, religion, and creed. We may be ready immediately to argue against an idea because it is being proposed by someone whose race or religion we do not like. The topic of the communication may have nothing to do with race or religion, but we do not feel that anyone with such antecedents can have ideas worth listening to. This is an obvious barrier to communication.

We may have a prejudice for or against someone because of his age or background. A teenager who feels that older people do not "understand him" could miss a useful idea because he refused to listen to a parent or teacher. By the same token, ideas coming from young people do not always get deserved attention from older people. A person who places great faith in formal education might be prejudiced against ideas coming from someone whose formal education is obviously lacking. In the opposite direction, the use of the phrase, "He's an egghead," may indicate a prejudice that handicaps effective listening.

You may feel a justifiable dislike for a person because of his past actions. But it does not necessarily follow that everything he has to say is based on poor ideas. A speaker's style may prejudice a listener for or against his ideas. You may not like someone's dress, his accent, his nervousness, or his apparent cockiness. If these influence your listening, you may miss important ideas or explanations that could be of value to you.

It is important in our listening that we hear the words, the ideas, and the development—not the man and our prejudice for or against him. There is no doubt that our later analysis may be influenced by the respect that he has earned or not earned, but we cannot know what he has said unless full attention has been given to him during the communication.

Mixing of fact and inference

Open a magazine to a picture and ask an individual to report what he sees. In most instances you will notice a mixture of fact and inference. He may report that there are three men in the picture (fact), but add that since it is an industrial scene and two men are in working clothes and one is in suit and tie, the latter is a boss of some kind (inference). He does not know who the man really is, but he makes an interpretation. He may report that one of the men has an expression of anger on his face when he does not really know what emotion the man felt. There are two cars in the picture, one of which has a crumpled fender; it is only inference to say that there has just been an accident.

Better still, ask two people who have attended a meeting at which a heated discussion took place to report to you what was said. Watch the mixing of fact and inference, and note how the latter will depend on who is making the report. There is nothing wrong with making inferences, but as a listener it is important for you to recognize what is fact and what is inference. If you accept inference for fact, your listening will obviously be colored. You might have to ask a number of questions to separate the facts and the inferences, but your listening will be highly improved if you are able to make distinctions of this nature, particularly on the important aspects of any communication.

Semantics

A discussion of the problem of word meanings has been included in Chapter 10. However, it is of great importance that the listener know the meaning of key words used by the speaker. Both the speaker and the listener will have definitions of such words as "educated person," "good teacher," "fine food," "democracy," "inexpensive weekend," and "fraternity." But how many of these meanings will be almost exactly the same? To one person a "good teacher" may mean a stimulating lecturer with high standards, while to someone else the phrase may mean one who tells lots of jokes or who never gives a grade lower than "C." "Fraternity" to some may mean a good place to live, eat, and have a good social program. To others it may mean the opportunity to give time and effort to help the brothers and the institution. Listening would be handicapped if such differences in meaning were present in the speaker and the listener.

It is important, therefore, that the listener determine the meaning of the key words used by a speaker. Failure to do this may result in misconceptions, or even a false idea of what the speaker is trying to achieve. The listener may be able to determine the meaning by carefully listening to the context in which the word or phrase is used. Failing that, the listener will want to ask the speaker certain questions either during or after the communication.

Inattention

A further human barrier to effective listening is ordinary inattention. Each of us has problems of his own, and unless the communicator is successful in inducing us to put these problems aside for the moment so that we can concentrate on his words, listening will suffer. It is the responsibility of the speaker to do all in his power to get the interest and attention of his listener, but it is equally incumbent on the listener to bend every effort to listen actively.

Sometimes it is possible to control the time of the communication. A roommate or friend may wish to communicate with you when your mind is fully occupied. You can explain the situation and ask for a postponement. You can decide not to bring up a certain problem at this committee meeting because you know that the group is tired or is concerned about another problem. It is often necessary, however, to listen carefully even though you are tired, or upset, or not in the mood. Inattention will obviously result in little meaning for you, so that you cannot afford the luxury of inattention at a given time.

Inattention may also be caused by poor communication. Even though the speaker is disorganized or has a poor delivery, he may have a great deal to say, and giving in to inattention too early could obscure valuable information.

ONE TECHNIQUE OF LISTENING

It is as important to have a pattern of listening as to have a pattern of speaking. Organization is important for the speaker, as has been pointed out frequently, and it is just as important for the listener. If you check your present pattern of listening you might discover that you listen sentence by sentence, idea by idea, or with no pattern at all. You may comprehend what is being said at any given time by these methods, but you probably cannot put the communication in any order. Thus, you can easily forget what has been said previously during the speech, and you will certainly have problems recalling the communication after it is over. For this reason, we must have some order to our listening, particularly since much of the communication we hear has no order in itself.

One simple listening pattern requires you to ask three questions while you are listening to a communication: (1) What does the speaker want? (2) Why does he want it? and (3) What support does he have for it?

What does the speaker want?

The first question concerns the focus of the communication. What is the purpose that the speaker is seeking, or what response does he want from me? Much of the communication that we listen to does not state a focus. The individual is reacting to something, and thus he begins to communicate "about" a topic. He has not analyzed the situation adequately to allow him to state a purpose. Still it is possible that he has one. He may be talking about Communism and Russia, and you, the listener, might be able to figure out that he feels that we have no definite foreign policy, or that we are too soft on Communism, or that our real worry is Red China, not Russia. Or he may be talking about fraternities on the campus, and you quickly know that he is unhappy with them. However, you must determine whether he wants to eliminate them, feels that they should change their function, or feels that the university should make some changes in their supervision.

If your listening is keyed to make such a determination, you may pick up many clues that would be missed if you were listening sentence by sentence with no key to tie them to. Of course, it may become obvious that the speaker has no focus but is merely talking all around a topic; and it is important also to know if this is true.

On some occasions, of course, the speaker will definitely state his focus and this will make the answer to the first question easy.

Why does he want it?

The answer to this question will concern the reasons that the speaker offers to support his focus. From the maze of statements that he makes about Communism and Russia you determine that he is trying to persuade you that we have no definite foreign policy and that we must have one if we are to be successful in the Cold War. You might then determine that his reasons for wanting a definite policy are: (1) The present policy is allowing the Communists to take the offensive in many parts of the world, (2) A defensive position makes us look weak in the minds of the people in these sections of the world.

The speech on fraternities might lead you to believe that the speaker believes that the fraternities should change their purpose and goal because: (1) the original purpose of fraternities ("social living," the speaker says) has been taken care of by university-built dormitories, and (2) the need today is to enhance the intellectual potential of brothers living in a chapter house.

In many communications these reasons will not be clearly stated by the speaker but must be determined by the listener. In many of the same communications, some of the main points may be discussed before the listener can determine the response that the speaker is seeking. If, however, the two questions, "What does he want?" and "Why does he want it?" are kept constantly in mind as the communication progresses, the pieces may fit together by the time the communication is over.

What support does he have for it?

This question concerns the speaker's evidence and reasoning. How well does he substantiate his reasons? Even in an organized communication this question will play a large role for the listener. In a rambling, disorganized presentation the speaker's evidence may be scattered throughout the communication. His reasoning may not be obvious, but with concentration, the listener may see the kind of reasoning he is employing.

Questioning the speaker's support can go a long way in helping the listener to determine the effectiveness of the communication. Are his reasons worthwhile as shown by the supporting evidence he presents? Are his reasons, if well supported, sufficient to justify the conclusion he desires? Many communications contain no support at all, but are instead comprised of a set of general statements. Other presentations that do not seem to have much evidence or reasoning involved are simply disorganized, and when what is said is tied to a couple of major points, there is considerable support for the contentions. The question of support is a listener's real basis for a judgment or evaluation.

ASK TWO TYPES OF QUESTIONS

After the speech has been analyzed by asking and answering these three questions, the listener is ready to pose some actual questions to the speaker. These questions are of two types: (1) questions to seek clarity, and (2) questions to assist in evaluating the communication.

Questions to seek clarity

The first task of the listener following a communication is to be sure that he got from the presentation what the speaker intended. This means asking questions to ascertain the correctness of his interpretation. Such questions might be, "Are you saying, then, that we have no definite foreign policy toward Communism?" "Were you indicating by what you just said that the goals of fraternities today are different from those of years ago, and that fraternities must change their purpose if they are to continue to exist?" "Do you feel that our lack of foreign policy gives Communism the offensive and makes us look bad in the eyes of many people?" "Do you feel that the original purpose of fraternities was to make a good social living atmosphere, but that today their purpose should be to assist the brothers in their intellectual pursuits?"

The speaker will then answer to report the accuracy of your judgment. He will say, "Yes, that is my main idea," or "You have understood most of what I meant, but I would add. . . ." By this interchange, you help to assure yourself as a listener that you have not missed his main purpose or the major points that he was developing. Without this type of questioning, many communicators are misunderstood. It makes little difference whether one places the blame on the speaker or on the listener; the result is not satisfactory. This problem might easily be solved with a simple question or two.

Whenever necessary and possible, therefore, a listener should quickly assure himself that he and the speaker agree on the speaker's purpose and the main reasons presented.

Questions for evaluation

Now comes the major task of the listener: he must arrive at a response based on the reasons and the supporting material presented by the speaker. He may wish to question the speaker further. He may ask questions concerning additional points not covered, such as, "Can we have a single foreign policy that meets all situations relative to Communism?" "Why are fraternities still a force on some university campuses?" This will give the speaker an opportunity to cover points not touched on in the presentation that have a bearing on the listener's belief or action.

Other possible evaluation questions concern the validity of

the reasoning or the sufficiency of the evidence. The speaker may omit certain supporting material because he did not think of it or because he did not consider it important. The listener may, however, need such material before he makes a decision or changes his attitude or belief. A question that pinpoints this need can quickly accomplish the goal.

This type of question can also point out that the speaker does not have sufficient evidence to arrive at the conclusion he holds. If he cannot support a point further when specifically asked for legitimate expansion, his communication deserves to be ineffective.

CONCLUSION

Although rhetoricians have discussed problems of effective speaking for centuries, effective listening has been studied only recently.

A listener may find it difficult to understand the true import of a communication if he lets his preconceived notions blot out a part of what is being said, if his prejudices render him incapable of accepting, if he makes inferences from what the speaker says and assumes that the speaker also proposed the inferences, if he interprets the words used by the speaker differently from the way they were meant, or if he does not pay enough attention to understand what is being said.

One pattern of effective listening involves asking three questions during a communication: What does the speaker want? Why does he want it? What support does he have for it? Answers to these questions attempt to identify the focus, organization, and supporting materials of the communication.

When a speaker has finished, a listener may ask him two kinds of questions. The first kind, which seeks clarity, asks the speaker what he meant by certain statements. The second kind of question, which asks for further evaluation, seeks information on related points not covered in the communication, or requests further information in substantiation of an idea propounded by the speaker.

REVIEW QUESTIONS

1. List five sources of "human static" that interfere with effective listening.

2. What three questions about the form and content of a communication form a guide to effective listening?

3. What two types of questions might the listener ask the speaker (either mentally or aloud) to clarify his understanding of what has been said?

PROJECTS

1. Choose a drawing or a picture that does not contain too many details. Send three students from the room, being sure that they do not see the picture. Now show the picture to the rest of the group and, after sufficient viewing, put it away, and choose a person to tell the group about the picture. Let the group make all the suggestions they desire to the speaker. Call one of the students back into the room, and let the speaker tell him about the picture. The student called back may ask any questions he wants. This person will then tell the second student called back, who will tell the third. The third student should tell the class about the picture as he makes a rough drawing of it on the board. All of this takes place in front of the group who remain quiet during the proceedings. Watch for:
   (a) inferences instead of facts
   (b) omission of important details
   (c) misunderstanding of words
   (d) how some individuals "fill in" details that they do not know

2. Have you ever turned on your radio in advance of a newcast, a weather program, or a sportscast that you wanted to hear, only to discover later that the program for which you had been waiting was about to conclude, and that you had no idea what was said? What are the implications of this experience for listening?

3. During an informal communication situation, make a list of the sounds that you hear that might interfere with the effectiveness

of your listening to what is being said. What are the implications for communication in this competition?

MATERIAL FOR THOUGHT AND DISCUSSION

Fortunately, I can suggest a little laboratory experiment which you can try to test the quality of your understanding. The next time you get into an argument with your wife, or your friend, or with a small group of friends, just stop the discussion for a moment and, for an experiment, institute this rule: "Each person can speak up for himself only *after* he has first restated the ideas and feelings of the previous speaker accurately and to the speaker's satisfaction."

You see what this would mean. It would simply mean that before presenting your own point of view, it would be necessary for you to achieve the other speaker's frame of reference—to understand his thoughts and feelings so well that you could summarize them for him. Sounds simple, doesn't it? But if you try it, you will discover that it is one of the most difficult things you have ever tried to do. However, once you have been able to see the other's point of view, your own comments will have to be drastically revised. You will also find the emotion going out of the discussion, the differences being reduced, and those differences which remain being of a rational and understandable sort. (*Carl R. Rogers and F. J. Roethlisberger, "Barriers and Gateways to Communication,"* Harvard Business Review, *July–August 1952, pp. 47–48.*)

On the St. Paul campus of the University of Minnesota each year the freshman class is tested for listening ability. When the tests are scored, the lowest 20 per cent of the class is given a twelve-week course in listening. At the end of the twelve weeks the entire freshman class is again tested for listening ability. In nearly every class it has been found that the low scorers on the first test have improved their listening ability after twelve weeks' training to the point where they equal or surpass the students who were not required to take the training. Every group of students that has taken listening training has improved at least 25 per cent in its ability to understand the spoken word. Some of the groups have improved as much as 40 per cent.

. . . .

. . . Why is the seemingly simple act of nondirective listening so difficult to accomplish? The best answer probably lies in the fact that such listening requires a kind of courage that few of us have ever mustered.

Whenever we listen thoroughly to another person's ideas we open ourselves up to the possibility that some of our own ideas are wrong. Most of us fight change, especially when it has to do with altering thoughts that may have been with us since childhood. Therefore, when we listen, something from inside makes us want to fight the change in our thinking that might be brought about by what we hear. "Hold on there," we are urged to say. "You must be wrong. That isn't the way I think. And you're not going to change my mind. I won't allow it. Now you listen to me." (*Ralph G. Nichols and Leonard A. Stevens,* Are You Listening? *New York: McGraw-Hill, 1957, pp. 15, 51–52.*)

(*The following two excerpts were written centuries apart. Quintilian wrote his* Institutes *about 96 A.D., and Blair first published his* Lectures *in 1783. Why are they placed at the end of the chapter on listening?*)

It has been my design to lead my reader from the very cradle of speech through all the stages of education which can be of any service to our budding orator till we have reached the very summit of the art. I have been all the more desirous of so doing because two books on the art of rhetoric are at present circulating under my name, although never published by me or composed for such a purpose. One is a two days' lecture which was taken down by the boys who were my audience. The other consists of such notes as my good pupils succeeded in taking down from a course of lectures on a somewhat more extensive scale: I appreciate their kindness, but they showed an excess of enthusiasm and a certain lack of discretion in doing my utterances the honor of publication. Consequently in the present work although some passages remain the same, you will find many alterations and still more additions, while the whole theme will be treated with greater system and with as great perfection as lies within my power. (*Quintilian,* The Institutio Oratoria of Quintilian, *tr. by H. E. Butler. Cambridge: Harvard University Press, 1953, Vol. 1, p. 9.*)

The following lectures were read in the university of Edinburgh, for twenty-four years. The publication of them, at present, was not altogether a matter of choice. Imperfect copies of them in manuscript, from notes taken by students who had heard them read, were first privately handed about; and afterwards frequently exposed to public sale. When the author saw them circulate so currently, as even to be quoted in print, and found himself often threatened with surreptitious publications of them, he judged it to be high time that they should proceed from his own hand, rather than come into public view under some very defective and erroneous form. (*Hugh Blair,* Lectures on Rhetoric and Belles Lettres. *Philadelphia: Matthew Carey, 1793, Vol. 1, p. iii.*)

12

The more discussion the better, if passion and personality be eschewed. Discussion, even if stormy, often winnows truth from error—a good never to be expected in an uninquiring age.

—William Ellery Channing

SMALL GROUP COMMUNICATION

It has frequently been said in this book that most communication takes place in the give-and-take situation where a few people discuss an idea. Some of these small groups are informal—in the dormitory, over coffee, before and after class, and in similar situations. Others will come about more formally in committees, organized meetings of extra-curricular groups, student government groups, protest groups, and the like. All of the concepts previously discussed apply to both types of situations, but a few suggestions may make communication in small groups even more effective.

SMALL GROUPS DEALING WITH PROBLEMS

Problems of various kinds are discussed by groups. The problem of what to do about a fellow student who makes too much noise in the dorm may come up in a bull session after dinner. A group, formal or informal, may discuss ways to help less fortunate members of the community. An organization may meet to choose a major project for the year, or to consider ways of interesting more students in their activity.

Many such sessions prove fruitless because each individual says what he wants to say when he wants to say it. The discussion goes off on various tangents with no results; or petty and irrelevant arguments consume most of the time so that little or no progress is made. The discussion concludes on a totally different topic from the one with which it began, and though many topics and problems have come up, no real attempt has been made to analyze or discuss any one of them.

If the small group desires to achieve any goal, some pattern or approach, however flexible, must be followed. One pattern that can be used in small group communication is: (1) to identify the problem, (2) to look for causes or reasons why the problem has arisen, and (3) to see if some solution can be found that overcomes the causes and alleviates the problem without bringing new and different troubles.

Identifying the problem

Sometimes the identification of the problem is simple: There is not enough money to sponsor a social program; a college rule forbids some action; membership has dropped so low the group can no longer be effective. On other occasions, however, the problem needs identification or definition before the group should proceed further. For example, in one university the students feel that parking is a problem. When asked what the problem is, they give various answers. Some students think that they should be able to park near all classroom buildings; others want a change in the regulation that prohibits freshmen from having cars on campus; still others want to drive on campus during class hours, which is forbidden. If these problems are all discussed at once, the communication will probably go in every direction with little achievement.

The same would be true of discussions on lack of student participation in outside activities, on student housing, on minority rights, and other issues. If students do not want to participate in outside activities, why should they? Perhaps the problem is that the student voice in college affairs will not be heard at the administrative level unless more students show interest. Is the problem of student housing that there is not enough housing, or that present housing is inadequately furnished, or that the rule against off-campus living is handicapping the student? Are you concerned with minority rights on the campus, in the state, or elsewhere? Unless all of the communicators in the small group are talking about the same thing, the prospects for effective communication are dim.

One procedure that might assist in identifying the problem is to determine the evil involved and whom that evil affects. If the parking, the housing, or the minority rights situation affects only a few and, while irritating, is no real handicap to anyone, the problem may not be worth discussing. If the situation does handicap certain individuals, the problem may be more easily identified once these individuals and the handicap they suffer have been clearly pointed out.

The proper limits, definitions, and identifications should be clear to everyone in the group before the discussion progresses farther.

Determining the causes

Generally, solutions are effective only when they overcome the causes that lead to the problem. A solution may sound fine and have appeal for the group but not really attack the basis of the problem. Such a solution will accomplish little. If the real cause of student apathy towards campus organizations is the concentration on academic work, it will do little good to add types of organizations in hopes that more will join. Rallies to gain support for minority rights may accomplish little if the individuals you want to influence feel that the present situation is satisfactory.

The determination of the true causes of a problem is often the most difficult step for a small group to take. Real analysis and communication are usually required to find the main reason or reasons. Because of the difficulty of this step, many communicators have a tendency to skip it altogether, or to assume too quickly causes or reasons that are not real. We are a solution-minded people; once a problem is posed, the first question usually asked is, "What can we do about it?" rather than, "What are the reasons for it?" Omitting this step has caused many poor solutions.

Finding the right solution

Discovering a solution is, of course, based on the previous step. The group is looking for a good solution that will alleviate the major causes of the problem without adding new difficulties to the situation. At times it is best for the group to collect all possible solutions before discussing any of them. This allows for a clear look at all, a possible combination of the best features of several solutions, and quick elimination of those that do not deal with the basic causes.

Once the causes are accurately determined, solutions may almost suggest themselves. If overcrowding is the real problem in dissatisfaction with housing, then one obvious solution is to provide more dormitory space. But if we are concerned about alleviating the problem here and now, for students already on campus, the most effective solution is not nearly so apparent.

It is also important to remember that the best solution in the world will be no solution if it is not put into practice. The real job of the small group is not finished when a solution has been discovered; the group must then discuss a plan of action to see that the solution is actually tried.

LEADERSHIP

Leadership is one of those words that everyone uses but few define. If you ask several people to define the term, some will say that the leader is the man who is appointed or elected to a position. Others will say that he is the most knowledgeable person in the group. Still others may answer that the leader is the man who channels ideas well, or keeps the group on the track. A leader may be any or all of these things. One definition of a leader is one who has the ability to influence others.

A good leader by his communication and action gets others to see a situation more clearly; he stimulates others to channel and control their energy to accomplish a satisfactory objective. He asks questions that clarify; he summarizes and makes transitions so that some pattern emerges. By all of these methods he is influencing others toward achievement of a common goal.

We often think of the person with the title of Chairman, President, or Manager as the leader. The title does not automatically make him a leader. The real leader in any group, formal or informal, is the person who at a given time is influencing others. The chairman of the committee may not be a leader at all. If no one assumes leadership, the committee will have a tendency to go off on tangents, follow no organized procedure, set no goals, and accomplish little. If, however, at any given time someone begins to influence the committee to concentrate on one aspect of a problem, to bring the proper issue and supporting material before the group, or to urge a certain action, he is the leader at that time. Leadership can change from person to person during a single small group communication. An individual's interest, his knowledge, or his communication skill may move him consciously or unconsciously to assume the leadership role at a particular time. Later in the discussion, if his interest wanes or someone else's knowledge proves superior, leadership might shift. The important idea is not to identify who is the leader but to make sure that the function of leadership is exercised and its purpose understood.

The leader keeps track of the discussion; he is sensitive to the need for identifying the most important aspects of a topic at a particular stage in the discussion. He will draw out the retiring member who has something to say, and as tactfully as possible try to cut off the windbag who likes to hear himself talk. When the discussion becomes repetitious, he summarizes what has been said and provides a transition into the next topic that should be given attention. Responsibility for this kind of leadership is shared by all; it cannot be left to the titular head.

If you assume the role of leader in a small group communication, consciously or unconsciously, you also assume certain heavy responsibilities. These responsibilities should be shouldered by all the communicators in the group, but because you are exerting greater influence at the time, they are more incumbent on you.

First, you must be sure that the goal you are striving for seems to have value. Do not get carried away by a feeling of power, but take special care to analyze matters more carefully so that you determine to the best of your ability that the chosen goal is worthwhile.

Second, be sure that you are fair to all in the group. Do not automatically rule out suggestions from those who approve your opinion, or even from a minority that seems out of step with the group. The only method of finding the best answers is to be sure that all sides of the question are discussed. This does not mean that you should try for balanced participation from all; some people may not have anything to contribute at a given time. However, your attitude, questions, and summaries must make it clear that all are free to contribute to the discussion.

Third, be aware of how much you talk. Do not monopolize the communication. Others in the group may have considered the question more deeply than you, so let them introduce their ideas. If you have a good point that is not being brought up by others, do not hesitate to state it. Make sure, however, that no one else is going to state the point before you do so. You will probably be talking enough with transitions, summaries, and questions, and if you introduce all of the new points also, others may lose interest.

THE USE OF QUESTIONS

Questions can play a major role in any communication situation, particularly in small groups. Most of the questions asked today in communication are not effective, however, because the various possibilities of this technique are not understood.

In Chapter 11 we discussed the use of questions for purposes of clarifying and evaluating ideas. Such questions as, "Do you mean . . . ?", "How do you define . . . ?", "Your two main reasons, then, are . . . ?", are valuable in all communication situations. There are other types of questions, however, that can also be of importance in communication.

In a small group where you are seeking information to arrive at a personal conclusion, questions can probe. A small group may be discussing the advisability of permitting students to exercise more influence on college policies by appointing student members to faculty-administration committees. At an appropriate time you might probe for information by asking, "What do you think would happen if students were placed on the Long-range Planning Committee of this institution?" In a discussion including faculty members, you might ask, "Would you compare and contrast the values of college study and work experience as it relates to your present position?" Too often our questions only skim the surface of a statement just made by others; at times we could make a better contribution to the group by asking a more probing question.

The answers to questions can often be used as launching points for further questions. Too often answers are interpreted as dividing a topic into pros and cons rather than seeking further information. If you ask a faculty member to compare and contrast college study and work experience as preparation for his job, a typical follow-up might be an attack on his answer. Perhaps further questions such as, "Why do you feel that . . . ?" or "Under what circumstances would you suggest the student interrupt his college career for work experience?" might shed much more light on the situation than an attack on a statement or idea that he developed in his answer. If a discussion becomes too much a choosing of sides on statements made by the participants, the results are lots of heat and little light.

All of this leads to the conclusion that questions should be thought through before they are asked. Stopping for adequate thought will help to determine what information is really needed, will assist in framing the question well, and will help you to evaluate whether the question should be asked or not.

If you do not stop to think, you may ask unnecessary or irrelevant questions, may frame them badly, and may not realize until later that the question should really never have been asked. All questions should be weighed in terms of what they will contribute to the desired result.

One other caution should be mentioned. Many people take questions personally, even though the questioner had no such intent in mind. They feel that almost any question challenges their knowledge, their honesty, or their ability to evaluate. They immediately go on the defensive, and their answers are aimed not at contributing to the over-all communication but at defending their own status, confidence, or reliability. This means that questions must be framed carefully so that no hint of personal charge is involved. Such a question as, "How can you believe that?" may be asked to elicit information, but it may be construed as an attack on the judgment of the earlier speaker. If framed differently: "That is an interesting point of view. What factors led you to that conclusion?" the question may bring a more informative answer. Some people will react emotionally no matter how the question is framed, but some care should be taken to reduce this possibility as much as possible.

ADDITIONAL REASONS FOR FAILURE

Pooling of ignorance

Perhaps the most common reason for failure of small group communication is that it becomes a pooling of ignorance. Informal groups often begin to discuss a topic of common interest with little previous thought on the part of the members, and much of the communication consists of personal opinion with little evidence or support. Perhaps few conclusions are reached by the group, but individual members may base a belief or an attitude on what is said. This happens also in more formally organized groups such as committees. The members gather at a certain time and place with no previous notice concerning what topics are to be discussed. As soon as a matter is introduced, the members begin to talk. It is soon obvious to an objective observer that little is being said that is a valid basis for analysis or action. Most of us seldom see this handicap in ourselves, however, and we continue to talk.

Two suggestions can be made to alleviate this problem. First, an agenda of the meeting can be announced when the members are notified of the meeting. Some of the communicators might give some thought and perhaps even study to the question before the meeting assembled. This would add to the success of the meeting. A formal agenda is not always necessary; even a suggestion about the topics to be discussed might suffice.

Second, do not be afraid to admit in any small group, formal or informal, that you, and perhaps others, do not have the requisite knowledge or have not given sufficient thought to the matter to make further discussion profitable at this time. The same people will be present on future occasions, and if, in the interim, profitable use is made of the time, better communication can result. As was pointed out in Chapter 4, if you have properly analyzed your knowledge and arrived at conclusions with proper support, you will be able to communicate in these meetings without previous notification. If notification of topics to be discussed is received, the same chapter discusses preparation procedures to follow even if you do not know the exact course the communication will take.

Concentrating on personalities

A second reason for failure in small group communication is that it often disintegrates into dealing with personalities rather than ideas. We have mentioned in this chapter the fact that questions are sometimes misinterpreted as attacking an individual rather than seeking information. This holds true also for the other communication of the group. Many people become more emotionally than mentally involved in discussions and forget the goal of the group, what point is being discussed at the time, and even what material has been presented. They become too much involved as people and communicate from their injured emotions. Nothing will make small group communication less effective.

This has happened to all of us—to some more than to others. If you will simply stop for a moment and ask what you are contributing to the desired results, or if someone not so emotionally involved will quietly point out what is happening, the emotion may subside to the point where communication can begin again. Often, however, everyone becomes so involved that no one steps aside to see what is happening and the communication is not only fruitless but often detrimental to further attempts.

Lack of pattern

A third important cause for small group communication failure has already been discussed in this chapter: the lack of following some type of pattern or procedure. One possible pattern has been mentioned here, but another may be used if it leads to worthwhile results.

In addition to these three cautions, remember what has been discussed in the previous chapters: know your listeners, be clear and concise, listen well, and adequately support a point of view—all good techniques in any communication situation.

CONCLUSION

Communication often takes place in small groups, formally or informally organized. In addition to what has already been discussed in this book, a few additional suggestions, particularly relevant to such situations, are made in this chapter.

Be sure that the group follows some flexible pattern of development. One such pattern is to (1) identify the problem, (2) determine the major causes or reasons for the problem, and (3) find a good solution aimed at overcoming the causes.

A leader can be defined as one who is influencing others by communication and action at any given time. This influence may come through questions, summaries, transitions, and introducing or supporting points. Leadership can change from time to time during a discussion and does not always stay with one person. Persons who assume leadership are not always aware of the fact. A good leader will constantly check the goal the group is striving toward to see whether or not it is worthwhile, will not override opposition, and will not monopolize the discussion.

Questions can be useful in small group communication. They help to clarify, evaluate, and probe deeper into a subject. Be sure to take time to consider the questions that you wish to ask, to ensure that they will be worthwhile and properly phrased.

Three special cautions are needed in small group communication: (1) do not let the discussion be a pooling of ignorance; (2) concern yourself with ideas and not with personalities alone; and (3) follow some pattern of procedure.

REVIEW QUESTIONS

1. What are three steps that might be followed to guide a group in seeking a solution to a problem?
2. Who is the real leader in a small group discussion?
3. What is the task of the leader?
4. What are the responsibilities of leadership?
5. List three good reasons for asking questions.
6. What are two dangers risked by questions that are not carefully thought through?
7. How can we guard against a pooling of ignorance in a discussion?

PROJECTS

1. Analyze a discussion that is held in your dorm or a committee to which you belong. Is there a pattern? Is support for ideas sufficient? How often are personalities the main problem?

2. Exert some leadership during a discussion in the near future. Were you effective? If not, what blocked your success? Did others begin to adapt to your method of procedure? Was anyone conscious of what you were doing?

3. Jot down five questions asked during a discussion in which you participate. Which made a contribution toward achieving the goals of the group? How could the others have been improved?

4. Most of you are not aware of the number of times you are involved in small group discussions. For a stated period of time (a day, three days, a week) keep a list of all of the occasions on which you join with several others (three or more) in attempting to explore an idea or come to a conclusion.

MATERIAL FOR THOUGHT AND DISCUSSION

I once asked a staff to make one word comments about

A surgeon who ordered an operation when the patient complained of a pain in the stomach before the source of the pain was located;
A judge who handed down his decision after the reading of the indictment;
A general who devised an invasion scheme without review of the intelligence reports;
A hunter who shot before sighting his quarry.

The words most mentioned were: reckless, stupid, unwise. Yet this same group considering a proposal for internal organization had given only five of the first fifty-one minutes of their talk to pinpointing the areas in which a change was needed. (*Irving Lee,* How To Talk With People, *New York: Harper & Row, 1952, pp. 61–62.*)

❖❖❖❖

All the behavior that goes on in a committee (or, indeed, in any verbal interchange) can be viewed as a sequence of questions, answers, and positive and negative reactions to the questions and answers. Three types of questions are distinguished: *asking for information, opinion,* and *suggestion.* Corresponding to these three types of questions are three types of answers: *giving information, opinion,* and *suggestion.* These answers are problem-solving attempts, and they call for reactions. Negative reactions include: *showing disagreement, tension,* or *antagonism.* On the positive side the corresponding reactions include: *showing agreement, tension release,* and *friendly solidarity.* These are the 12 categories of remarks used as a basis of analysis in the Harvard experiments.

. . . .

The laboratory findings, while still tentative, indicate that the man who is judged by the group members to have the "best ideas" contributing to the decision is *not* generally the "best-liked." There are two separate roles—that of task leader and that of social leader. If a man comes into a task-leadership position because he is popular or best liked, he is ordinarily confronted with a choice: (1) If he chooses to try to keep the task leadership of the group, he tends to lose some of his popularity and to collect some dislikes. (2) If he chooses to try to keep his popularity, he tends to lose the task leadership. People differ in the way they solve this dilemma, although most tend to prefer to keep the popularity rather than the task leadership.

The difficulty becomes more acute with time. At the end of the group's first meeting there is 1 chance in 2 that the task leader will be the most liked. At the end of the second meeting the chances are reduced to 1 in 4. At the end of the third they are 1 in 6, and at the end of the fourth they are only 1 in 7.

There are apparently few men who can hold both roles; instead, the tendency is for these positions to be held by two different men. Each is in reality a leader, and each is important to the stability of the group. The task leader helps to keep the group engaged in the work, but the pressure of decision and work tends to provoke irritation and injure the unity of the group. The best-liked man helps to restore this unity and to keep the members of the group aware of their importance as particular individuals, whose special needs and values are respected. These men complement each other, and they are both necessary for smooth operation of a committee. (*Robert*

F. Bales, "In Conference," Harvard Business Review, *March–April 1954, pp. 45, 47.)*

As the father of five, I know that today's young are remarkably realistic and deeply committed to the building of a better society than that in which we live. They may be children, but they will not fool themselves and they will not permit themselves to be fooled. The happiest and most productive youths I know today are those who are engaged in the civil rights struggle, frequently under the auspices of a religion. Some have even been martyrs.

The youths I know believe this action is relevant and meaningful, and those who are religious accept this activity as the ultimate and supreme manifestation of their religions in today's world. They have undertaken to deal with their fellow men no longer as objects, but as subjects, as human beings. They have sought to establish and are establishing an I-Thou relationship, not only with their fellow man, but with their God. They are communicating, not only by means of words with human beings whom they hold in respect, but also by means of deeds, with the dignity which the human personality deserves. They understand what many of an older generation have forgotten, that a dialogue requires not only that we speak, but that we *listen* as well.

Strangely enough, this idea is encompassed in an ancient chant of my people, which is heard at every service, and has been heard at every service for 5000 years wherever Jews have worshipped: "Hear, O Israel, the Lord our God, the Lord is one," and the word, "hear," the Rabbis say, means "listen"! *(From an address by Morris B. Abram, President, American Jewish Committee, to the Fifth General Synod of the United Church of Christ, Chicago, July 5, 1965.)*

INDEX